Resounding The Psalms
David Potter

Resounding The Psalms
David Potter

Dedicated to my wife, Anne with thanks for her support and steadfast love

©David Potter 2016

Introduction

This is how I have heard The Psalms, these poems of praise and lament. The psalmist's cry for help and recognition, a nation's prayer of repentance and their call for justice. They cover the whole range of human emotions from joy to anger, from hope to despair.

The Psalms may sit in the middle of the Old Testament but their language and themes permeate the whole of the Bible. They foretell the coming of the Messiah, they call for the forgiveness of sin, they praise God as creator and redeemer and recognise His priorities to care for the poor and hungry, to look after the immigrant and protect the widow and dispossessed. Their verses are quoted by Jesus and echoed by Paul. Unsurprisingly, they continue to be used in Jewish worship and the words and poetry of The Psalms is found in Christian liturgy, as well as being recited as Holy Scripture.

The Psalms can be a challenge to read and to fully understand. They are full of emotion, and private anguish. These hymns or prayers set down the psalmist's spiritual and bodily concerns, usually in the context of the history of God's chosen people. The Psalms also provide us with unforgettable images of the glory and majesty of God's power and creation. Here we have the psalmist in conversation with God, often arguing and calling for his intervention to save the writer or to save Israel.

At times, the psalmist sounds selfish, like a demanding child, calling on God for special attention, even when the psalmist acknowledges his own shortcomings. He pleads for God's help, he tells God what to do, he rails against his enemies, and he generally feels sorry for himself. Elsewhere, the psalmist glorifies all that God has done, both in his power over creation but also in guiding and saving the people of Israel throughout their history.

This is my own take on the 150 poems. By no means a faithful translation, rather an interpretation of other versions, put in my own voice. A poetic response to the call they make to our worship and prayer.

Resounding The Psalms

Psalm 1: Joyful in the Lord

Walk joyfully in the light of the Lord
And meditate on His laws.
Follow the safe path He has made for us,
Set beside streams of living water,
Where trees prosper and bring forth fruit in their season,
Their perfect leaves never wither.
But there is no safe way for sinners to take
For the wind of God will blow them away.
Be confident that the Lord watches over the righteous.

Psalm 2: God's promise

The Lord laughs at those who would plot against Him
Against Him and His anointed.
God has made a promise to us,
He has sent His Son to rule the earth.
Let this be a warning to those who might oppose Him,
Fall down before the Son of God; put your trust in Him.
Blessed are they who put their trust in God.

Psalm 3: A shield to protect me

My troubles surround me
But the Lord sets a shield to protect me.
The Lord answers all my calls of anguish and alarm,
The Lord sustains me.
He gives me courage to face all my difficulties,
With the promise of deliverance.
His rich blessings are bestowed upon His joyful people.

Psalm 4: Let His light shine

Answer my prayer, Lord; answer me when I call to you.
Stand before the Lord in awe and do not sin against Him,
Put your trust in the Lord; let His light shine upon you.
Be glad that you can lie down and sleep in safety.

Psalm 5: Trust in God

Hear my words, O Lord, hear my morning prayer
As I sigh and plead my case to you.
You hate all evil and all evil doers,
Your steadfast love makes a straight way for me to follow
Away from the deceit and false counsels of my enemies
Let us rejoice and ever sing for joy that we can find our refuge in you.

Psalm 6: Weary with moaning

Merciful Lord, be gracious to me in my anguish.
I dwell in terror and am wrung out with exhaustion,
Weary with my moaning and weeping.
But the Lord has heard my cry
The Lord has heard my prayer
And I shall be healed.

Psalm 7: Establish the righteous

Lord, you are my protector and my refuge
My place of safety, justice and judgement.
Strike down my enemies in your anger,
Build up and establish the righteous.
Let the wicked plotters fall into their own trap,
Save those who are upright in heart.
Sing praises to the Lord because he is good.

Psalm 8: The glories of creation

O Lord, how majestic is your name in all the earth!
The glories of your creation are staggering
Yet you have given men and women the privilege
Of dominion over the works of your hands.
How majestic is your name in all the earth!

Psalm 9: Judgement and justice

I will give thanks to the Lord with my whole heart and exult His wonderful name
For his judgement is righteous and my enemies stumble before Him.
He judges the world with justice and those who know the Lord put their trust in Him.
The needy and the oppressed will not be ignored; the hopes of the poor will not be forgotten,
O Lord, let the nations know that they will be judged, let the nations tremble.

Psalm 10: To help the needy

O Lord, where are you when you are needed most?
The wicked think they can hide their sins from you.
Through many acts of greed and oppression
They murder the innocent and defile goodness.
They believe they will not be brought to account.
But Lord, you will come to the help of the needy.
You will do justice for the orphan and the oppressed.
Rise up, O Lord; O God lift up your hand.

Psalm 11: Vulnerable

In the Lord I take my refuge for I am vulnerable
God beholds the actions of humankind
He tests the righteous and the wicked
He dispenses justice and the upright shall behold his face
Trust in God and you will be saved.

Psalm 12: Surrounded by the ungodly

Lord, help the dwindling band of righteous people.
We are surrounded by the ungodly,
Their words are deceitful, their mouths filled with empty boasting.
But the Lord is on hand to protect the worthy
To put us in a place of safety and guard us against evil.

Psalm 13: Abandoned

Am I forgotten, Lord? Have you hidden your face from me?
For how long will this go on, how long must I suffer this rejection?
If you do not shine your light on me, my enemies will prevail,
But I trust in your steadfast love and I will sing to the Lord.

Psalm 14: Impunity

Fools say there is no God, they deny their own salvation.
They think they can sin with impunity but they are wrong.
God will deliver those who are in peril from evil doers,
He will rescue Israel and restore the fortunes of His people.

Psalm 15: God's sanctuary

Who may dwell in God's sanctuary?
Those who do what is right,
Who show respect and love for their neighbour,
And stand by their faith, even when it hurts.
Those who fear the Lord.
These will dwell in God's sanctuary.

Psalm 16: God's presence

Protect me, O God; I have no good beside you.
You are my chosen portion, my salvation.
Day and night I keep the Lord always before me.
Heart and soul I rejoice for the path of life you show me.
I give thanks for the joy of being in your presence.

Psalm 17: My cause

O Lord, hear the goodness of my cause,
I have not strayed from your paths.
You have examined my heart,
You have tested my inmost thoughts,
The words from my lips do not lie.
Incline your ear to me and hear my words
For I seek your steadfast love to give me refuge.
Guard me and protect me from wickedness,
The wickedness that rages all around me.
Rise up, O Lord, and be my deliverance,
Your presence will be my reassurance and my relief.

Psalm 18: Tower of strength

My love is in the Lord
He is a tower of strength for me, a sure foundation for my life.
I call upon the Lord with praises,
Confident that he will deliver me from my enemies.
I have been through many deep sorrows and tribulations,
God heard my cry for help and He acted swiftly to save me.
The earth shook at His approach
And the clouds parted with the brightness of His presence.
He scattered my enemies and reached down to rescue me.
I have been faithful to the Lord's wishes
And he has repaid me with His blessings.
Lord, you show mercy to those who are themselves merciful,
You give blessings to the pure in heart and deliver the humble.
You light up my darkness so that I can see my way clearly.
God is perfect, a sure haven for all who believe.
He has given me the rock of His salvation,
A wide path for my steps so that I will not stumble.
The Lord lives! Blessed be the God of my salvation.

Psalm 19: Heavens declare

The heavens declare the glory of God,
By day and night they proclaim the wonders of His handiwork.
God guides us by His perfect laws to ways of justice and light.
Laws that are better than gold and sweeter than honey,
That warn us away from harm and give success to those who obey them.
But what of the sins in my heart?
Cleanse me from my hidden faults.
Let my words and my thoughts be acceptable to you,
O Lord, my rock and my redeemer.

Psalm 20: Boast in the Lord

When you are beset with troubles, may the Lord be with you and comfort you.
May God recognise you as a true and faithful servant and may He smile upon you
So that we can shout for joy at your deliverance.
Some boast of earthly success but our boast is in the Lord our God.

Psalm 21: Rich blessings

We rejoice in your strength, O Lord, and in your generosity.
So many rich blessings you have bestowed upon us
And we delight in your steadfast love.
You will be victorious over evil.
Be exalted, O Lord, for all your glorious power!

Psalm 22: Forsaken

My God, my God, why have you abandoned me?
You are so far away, you cannot hear my groans.
You do not answer my cries for help;
Yet you are holy and have reached out to save your people in the past.
But I am most unworthy, mocked and despised by all;
Lord, how you have helped me before!
You kept me safe when I was young and I have depended on you,
Don't leave me now, when I am in the greatest danger. No one else can help.
I am surrounded by my worst fears, the most hostile situations
And I am at my weakest and lowest ebb; I am drained of strength and courage.
Lord, don't delay; rescue me from my suffering, save me from death.
I will tell of your name widely, you who seek the Lord, praise him!
All the ends of the earth shall remember and turn to the Lord.
All who are mortal shall worship Him,
Generations as yet unborn shall hear of all He did for us.
I will praise you, O Lord.

Psalm 23: Still waters

I follow the good shepherd who gives me all I need.
I am led to graze in green pastures and walk beside still waters
I am uplifted and joyful as he walks beside me on safe paths.
Even on the darkest journey or in the wildest places I fear no evil.
The shepherd protects and comforts me,
He prepares a table before me in the sight of my enemies
He anoints my head with oil and I am completely satisfied.
Surely such blessings will be mine all the days of my life
And I shall dwell in the house of the Lord forever.

Psalm 24: Fling open wide the gates

The earth is the Lord's and all who dwell in it.
Only those who are pure in heart may ascend to the Lord,
Where they will receive God's blessings.
Make way for the King of glory, fling open wide the gates,
For the Lord approaches
The Lord of Hosts is mighty and strong.

Psalm 25: Teach me your paths

O Lord, I put my trust in you, do not fail me.
Show me your way, O Lord, teach me your paths.
Forget the sins of my youth and look on me with mercy and forgiveness.
God is good and he will welcome those who humbly turn to him.
Show me your loving mercy, Lord, for I am overwhelmed and in deep distress.
See my sorrows, feel my pain, forgive my sins.
Deliver me from the perils that surround me.
Let Godliness and Truth protect me as I wait for you, Lord.

Psalm 26: Constant in my worship

Judge me, test me, prove me, O Lord, for I have been faithful to you.
I choose my company carefully and do not mix with sinners
I am constant in my worship and wash my hands to prove my innocence.
I walk in truth and piety, be gracious to me Lord and show your steadfast love to me.
I stand on level ground and proclaim your righteous name to all.

Psalm 27: My stronghold

The Lord is my light and my salvation, whom shall I fear?
Because He is my stronghold my enemies will stumble and fall.
All I want is to stay in the house of the Lord forever,
To delight in the beauty of the Lord and the glories of His dwelling place.
There I will be safe from my foes and I will sing praises with much joy.
Do not turn away from me, O Lord, do not forsake me.
Make it plain what I must do and lead me to safety on a level path.
Wait patiently for the Lord; be confident that He will hear your prayers.

Psalm 28: My Strength and shield

I lift up my hands to heaven and cry out for help.
Do not punish me with the wicked ones who deserve their sentence
Praise the Lord for he has listened to my pleadings
He is my strength and my shield against all dangers
Defend your people, Lord and lead them like a good shepherd.

Psalm 29: Praises and blessings

Sing praises to the Lord, worship His might and majesty.
The voice of the Lord thunders through the skies and over the waters
The earth responds with joy in recognition of His voice.
From the beginning, God has showed his mastery over all creation
He will bless His people with peace and strength.

Psalm 30: Clothed with joy

I praise you, Lord, for you have rescued me from my enemies
You have healed me and given me back my life.
Join me in singing praises to the Lord and give thanks for his holy name
His anger lasts a moment but his love lasts forever.
Without your blessings I was lost and useless,
But when you turned back to me my sorrow became joy.
You have clothed me with joy and I will go on praising you forever.

Psalm 31: I put my trust in the Lord

For me, Lord, you are a strong fortress and a place of safety.
Rescue me from the net that has been set to ensnare me
I have put my complete trust in the Lord to deliver me from danger and set me free.
Be gracious Lord for I am in distress and my life is spent with sorrow
I am shunned by those I know and an object of derision to all
But I put my trust in the Lord to uphold the righteous.
Your abundant goodness and steadfast love will be a refuge for all who are faithful.
I had drifted far from God but he heard my supplications when I cried out for help.

Psalm 32: Joy in forgiveness

There is joy in the forgiveness of the Lord, relief for those who have confessed their sins.
When I hid my sin in silence I felt the Lord's hand heavy on my soul and I dried up.
What relief when I realised my error and acknowledged my sins to God
This is a lesson for all the faithful to learn, to find deliverance whilst there is still time.
Follow my example, steadfast love surrounds those who trust in the Lord.
So rejoice in the Lord and shout for joy all you who seek His forgiveness.

Psalm 33: Sing a new song

Sing to the Lord a new song of praise and joyfulness,
On every instrument play to the greatness of God.
For He is most worthy of our trust and praise,
By his tender word the earth and the heavens were formed
At his command the waters were poured into oceans
We are humbled by the power and beauty of his creation.
Whilst the intentions of men and women can come to nothing,
God's plan lasts forever; He is the same for every generation.
The Lord watches over those who love him, He is our shield and our redeemer.
Our heart sings out for the goodness of the Lord.

Psalm 34: To be Worthy of the Lord

I will bless the Lord at all times; I will constantly sing His praises,
I will boast the mercy he has shown to me and exult his holy name,
For he answered my prayers and released me from all my fears.
Others also testify to His greatness, they shine with his glory.
See the Lord is great, and happy are those who take refuge in Him.
Come, let me teach you to be worthy of the Lord
Keep your tongue from evil and your lips from deceit
Stay away from wickedness and do only good.
Strive to live in peace with everyone.
The Lord watches over the righteous and he will hear their cries.
The Lord is very near, to console the broken hearted and revive the downcast.
The faithful do not escape troubles but God is your strength at such times
He redeems his followers; those who take their refuge in Him will be saved.

Psalm 35: Battle against my enemies

Lord, join me and others in the battle against my enemies.
I am hard pressed and I need to hear you say you will save me.
Confound the plans of those who are against me, drive them away.
I will rejoice in the Lord because he will rescue me,
You protect the weak from the strong and the poor from those who would rob them.
I have been wrongly accused, my sympathy has been repaid with malicious mocking
Rescue me from my treacherous enemies and I will proclaim my thanks.
My enemies bear false witness against me, but you have seen the truth, O Lord.
Rise up, O Lord my God, vindicate me, and stand in my defence.
Do not let them say "We have swallowed you up."
Shame those who boast against me and who rejoice at my troubles.
Let us be glad and say "Great is the Lord who cares for His children."

Psalm 36: Constant love

For those who continue to sin there can be no relationship with God,
They flatter themselves with their own company and their own deeds,
They have no respect and are set on a downward path of mischief and deceit.
Your steadfast love, O Lord, fills all creation; your goodness extends to all,
All people are welcome to take refuge under the shadow of your wings.
You are the fountain of life and our light is from your light.
We build our relationship with you, O Lord, through your constant love.

Psalm 37: The humble will inherit

Have no regard for the wicked, they will soon wither and fade away like grass.
Trust in the Lord and do good, delight in the Lord and you will have everything you desire.
Commit yourself to the Lord and you will shine as his disciple, as bright as the noonday sun.
Wait patiently for the Lord to act, do not be envious of those who seem to prosper.
Stay calm, do not fret, in a little while all will be well and the humble will inherit every blessing.
Although the wicked plot against the godly they will not succeed, their attacks will fail,
The Lord has seen their iniquity and the evil shall perish and disappear like smoke.
Those blessed by the Lord shall inherit the earth, but those cursed by him shall die.
He directs the way of the faithful, delights in every step and holds them up if they should stumble.
Throughout my life I have never seen the righteous forsaken or their children go hungry.
The Lord loves justice and fairness, he will never abandon his people, they will be kept safe.
God's people shall inherit the land set aside for them and will live there forever.
Don't be impatient for the Lord to act! Travel in hope and in due season he will reward you.
I have seen the wicked in great power looming over us but God has vanquished them.
The Lord saves the godly; he is their salvation and refuge when trouble comes.

Psalm 38: Racked with guilt

O Lord, do not punish me in your wrath. Your anger strikes deep and I feel crushed
Your indignation has wounded me and broken my body. I groan in despair.
My senses fail me, I am racked with pain, disease and loathing permeate my body.
My enemies seek to take advantage of my weakness and plan treachery against me.
I am waiting and praying for you, O Lord my God, come and protect me.
How often I find myself on the verge of sinning, such terrors confront me.
I confess my sins, I am sorry for what I have done, it is a great sorrow for me.
My enemies persecute me by repaying evil for the good path I try to follow,
Do not forsake me Lord, come to my aid quickly, my saviour.

Psalm 39: A few more heartbeats

I had resolved to put a guard on my tongue, to stop myself from a complaining,
But it was all to no avail and there came a point when I could keep quiet no longer!
I pleaded with God to let me know how much time I have left, how many more days.
It is such a short span, just a few more heartbeats.
My whole life is only a moment in the sight of God.
And now, Lord, what do I wait for? My only hope is in you. Deliver me from my sins.
I am fragile and exhausted, frail as breath; when you punish a man for his sins he is destroyed.
I am a traveller in this place, I will soon be gone, hear my cry, see my tears.
Spare me, Lord! Let me recover and be filled with happiness before I die.

Psalm 40: Written on my heart

I waited patiently for the Lord and he bent his head to me and heard my cry.
He lifted me out of my life's desolate pit and set my feet on a firm path.
He gave me a new song to sing, a song of praise to our God.
To worship the glorious things he has done, a song to encourage others to put their trust in God.
O Lord my God, none can compare with your wondrous deeds and your loving kindness.
You have no need for sacrifices and burnt offerings; what you want is my life-long service.
See, here I am, Lord, I delight to do your will for your law is written on my heart.
I have told everyone the good news that you forgive people's sins. I have made no secret of this.
O Lord, don't hold back your tender mercies from me! My hope is in your love and faithfulness.
My many sins have caught up with me and I am ashamed to look you in the face.
Please, Lord, rescue me! Make haste to help me. I am poor and needy, save me.

Psalm 41: Where do I stand in God's mercy

God blesses those who remember the poor.
He helps them out of their troubles.
He protects and rewards them,
Sustains and heals them, nurses them when they are sick.
And what of me, where do I stand in God's mercy?
For I have sinned.
My enemies have no compassion for me.
They act friendly but spread mischief abroad.
They think my days are numbered,
That I will never rise out of my bed again.
My friends desert me but don't you desert me, Lord.
Remember me in my troubles.
You have saved me because I have been honest.
Blessed be the Lord, forever and ever. Amen

Psalm 42: Forsaken

As the deer pants for cool streams, so my soul longs after you, O God.
My soul thirsts for God, for the living God. When shall I behold the face of God?
I weep for his help day and night and my enemies taunt me with my cries.
I take courage from remembering the great processions and festivals in the Temple.
I can be sure there will yet be new opportunities to praise and worship you, O Lord.
And I remember all your blessings on this lovely land, the deep beauty of cataract and mountain.
These all flood over me, yet, day by day, the Lord also pours out his steadfast love upon me.
At night, God has a song of comfort for me and I pray to God who gives me life.
O God, my rock, why have you forsaken me. Why must I suffer these taunts from my enemies?
O my soul, don't be discouraged. God will act. The time will come when I will again praise his name.

Psalm 43: Stand with me

Stand with me, God, and defend my cause,
Against the ungodly, the deceitful and the unjust.
I take my refuge in you, but why have you cast me off
And left me stranded and depressed?
Send your light and truth to lead me back to you,
Then I will go to the altar of God and praise you with the harp, O God, my God.
O my soul, don't be discouraged. God will act.
The time will come when I will again praise his name.

Psalm 44: Risks in being faithful

O God, we have heard of all your marvellous deeds in the past.
Our ancestors have told us how you drove out the alien nations and gave it all to us.
This was only possible with your help,
You favoured our forefathers with your mighty power.
You are my King and my God;
It is only by your strength and by your name that we have victory.
Our constant boast is God; we will give thanks to your name forever.
But now you have abandoned us and have not helped us in our battles
You have even helped our enemies to find our weak points and to scatter our people
You have sold us cheaply,
We are mocked by our neighbours and we have lost our self esteem.
All this has happened, Lord, despite our loyalty to you.
We have remained true to your covenant.
Our hearts remain committed to you, Lord.
We have not left the path you set for us.
God knows everything; He would discover any transgressions,
He knows the secrets of the heart.
Following God puts us in danger,
For there are risks in being faithful to the Lord.
Wake up! Rouse yourself, O Lord,
Do not let us be cast off forever.
Why do you not see our oppression?
Why do you choose to ignore our infliction?
We sink down in the dust, face down in the mud.
Rise up, O Lord, and come and help us.
Save us by your constant love.

Psalm 45: The bridegroom

My heart calls out to me to write a love song to the Lord:
You are the most fair and your words bring comfort and delight to all,
You will be victorious in your battle to defend truth, humility and justice.
You love what is good and hate what is wrong and evil. Go forth in majesty!
All around you is a celebration of joy and happiness, rich colours and loud music.
You are dressed as the bridegroom and the world hurries to be your bride.
Your name will be honoured by all generations; the nations will praise you forever.

Psalm 46: He only has to speak

God, whatever happens, you will always be our refuge and our strength.
The mountains may fall and the seas overwhelm us but you will be there to save us.
God is the constant centre of peace and tranquillity, despite the turmoil in the world,
He only has to speak and the violence of the earth subsides, the nations submit.
God, the commander of heaven and earth, is here to rescue us.

Psalm 47: Call all people

Clap your hands and shout for joy to celebrate the Lord our God.
He is wonderful beyond words, sing out your praises to our King.
God is king of all the earth and he reigns over the nations from His holy throne.
Call all people of the world to join in praising God for they surely belong to Him.

Psalm 48: Mighty love

How great is the Lord and most worthy of our praise.
He shines out over all the earth as He defends His people.
Mighty are your works for our salvation, though we are so unworthy.
The story of the love you have for your people is precious to us,
We wonder at your faithfulness to us and we worship your holy name.
The citadel of the Almighty is a glorious place to behold,
We are uplifted in our spirit to know that God, who is so mighty, loves each one of us.

Psalm 49: Justice in the end

I have a great truth to tell everyone who will listen, an insight that all need to know.
When troubles come, you do not need to worry, it is not a matter of wealth or position.
Such matters cannot make the ransom payment for a misspent life.
God's forgiveness cannot be bought; a soul is far more precious than that.
Whatever your standing in society, whatever your worldly value,
Such matters have to be left behind at the threshold of death.
Death is the shepherd and destiny of all mankind,
In the morning will come the reckoning and the evil will be slaves to the good.
So do not be dismayed when troubles come for there will be justice in the end.

Psalm 50: Worthy sacrifice

The whole world, east and west, hears the summons of Almighty God,
A call that comes with devastating fire and a raging storm.
He has come to judge his faithful people, to administer his justice.
It is not our sacrifices of flesh and blood that God wants, for all creatures are his,
He wants our sacrifice of thanksgiving and our promises of faithfulness fulfilled,
To show trust in times of trouble so we will give glory for his salvation.
True praise is a worthy sacrifice that brings honour to God.
Those who walk with God along his paths will find salvation.

Psalm 51: A sinner

I have sinned, forgive me, Lord, it is a stain on my soul.
I have sinned, wash me, Lord, cleanse me from my guilt.
I have sinned, save me, Lord, let me be pure again.
I was born a sinner; create in me a new clean heart, O God.
Do not drive me away from you or take your Holy Spirit from me.
Help me to return to you, to know the joy of your fellowship once more.
I crave your forgiveness and I will sing the praises of your justice.
My sacrifice is a sincere and humbled spirit, a heart yearning for your love.
When my heart is made right with you then all things will be possible in your name.

Psalm 52: Cruel gossip

I know of the people who boast of their wickedness,
Plotting their treachery all day long,
With cruel gossip and slanderous talk you despise God
And trust in your own lies.
But God will easily bring you down to earth
And settle your account.
But I am like an olive tree sheltering in God's garden,
Protected by the Lord himself.
I trust in the love and mercy of God forever and ever.
I will praise the Lord for what he has done for me and glorify his name.

Psalm 53: Faithful follower

Only a fool would think there is no God,
Only a fool with a wicked heart.
God searches for the righteous,
But he cannot find one faithful follower, not one.
Are their lives not empty and barren,
Those who never call upon God?
There will be a time when they will have need of God,
But God will have rejected them.

Psalm 54: Your mighty name

The power of your mighty name will save me
From those who want to attack me,
Those who give no thought to God.
But God is my helper, my constant companion.
The violence of my betrayers will rebound on them.
Silence them with your truth, O Lord,
I will praise your name, O God, for it is good.

Psalm 55: Wings of a dove

I need you to hear my plea, O Lord; do not hide from my prayers.
I am desperate for you to respond to my plight,
To save me from my enemies who surround and terrorise me.
I am overwhelmed with fear and trembling, no way to turn.
If I could fly away, I would escape to distant lands
O that I had the wings of a dove.
Lord, sow discord amongst my enemies,
Bring down their defences with their own wickedness and treachery.
The heart of their city is filled with violence and spite.
I was betrayed by a friend who spoke peace but wanted war,
We walked together and his words were sweet, but underneath razor sharp.
Let death strike them down, let them perish in confusion.
I will call on the Lord to save me, I will offer up my prayers continually.
I am confident that the Lord will answer my prayers.
Hand over all your troubles to the Lord, he will carry all your burdens.
He will hold up the godly, he will not let them stumble.
I am trusting in the Lord to save me.

Psalm 56: Exchanged promises

Be gracious to me, Lord, have mercy on me.
I feel hemmed in and oppressed, pressed down low.
O God, appear on high and cast my fears down to the ground.
You have seen my tremors at night, counted my tears each day.
I call on you to turn back the shadows and answer my lament.
I will be defiant because I know that God is on my side,
He will bring light to my darkness and I will not be afraid.
I have exchanged promises with God and we will stay true to one another,
He has brought me salvation and allowed me to walk in his presence.

Psalm 57: To Sing Praises

Lord, there is a storm coming,
But I will take refuge under your wings until it is passed.
My enemies are ready to entrap me with their lies and treachery,
Lord, rise up on high, glorious and powerful, to shine over all the earth.
My heart is steadfast, O God, and I will sing your praises,
Let me find the words and the music to greet the new day with a song.
I will proclaim the goodness of the Lord to all nations,
For your unfailing love is wider than the heavens,
You faithfulness higher than the skies,
Let your glory shine over all the earth.

Psalm 58: What is justice?

Who truly knows the meaning of justice?
Do any of us deal fairly with one another?
Some even go so far as to turn it on its head
And in their hearts devise injustice and mete out violence!
Poisonous as deadly snakes that cannot be tamed,
Striking deep and sharp with their fangs!
O God, make them disappear, like water on parched earth,
Make their crooked dealings useless in their hands.
The just rejoice when right overcomes such evil,
Everyone will know that good is rewarded,
That there is a God who does justice here on the earth.

Psalm 59: No case against me

Rescue me, Lord, for I am in great danger,
Protect me from those who are poised ready to attack me.
The powerful band together against me,
They have fabricated their case against me
For I have done no sin, no wrong against them.
I hear them prowling in the night and using your name in vain,
Thinking they are safe from detection,
But you, Lord, hear and see everything,
I turn to you to come to my aid.
Stagger my enemies with your power and bring them low,
Let them slink back into the night where they belong.
I will sing of your strength and proclaim your love,
For you are my stronghold in the day of my distress.

Psalm 60: Tremble to our depths

Lord, you have become angry with us
And broken down our defences,
We have fallen out of your favour
And you no longer lend us your support.
We are torn apart without your love,
We tremble to our very depths.
Now is the time to rally around your banner,
To seek your truth.
You will lead us to safety, Lord,
Rescue us from the clutch of our enemy.
God has long vowed to help us
And promised that the victory will be ours.
Return again to save us, O Lord, for without you we are useless.
With God on our side we will feel whole again,
With His help we will do mighty things.

Psalm 61: My Distant Voice

Although I might seem a long way from you, Lord, hear my prayer.
However faint my heart beat, however distant my voice, hear my call.
Lead me from wilderness
To the safety of your fortress tower,
Let me find shelter in your presence,
In a high and holy place of refuge.
O God, you know that I have vowed to praise you every day
And you have given me the same blessings you give to all who love you.
Send your loving kindness and truth to guard and watch over me,
I will not forget my vow to praise your name every day.

Psalm 62: Refuge

Only in God do I find my salvation,
Only in him does my soul find rest.
He is my rock,
Where I can stand firm in my faithfulness,
He is my refuge,
Where I can find rest and replenishment.
The tottering wall of my own defences
Is replaced by God's strong fortress
The crumbling fence of my own will
Is replaced by God's steely resolve.
We can trust in God always,
Pour out our hearts to the Lord and he will listen.
Do not be tempted away from his side
By riches or vain promises of power.
God is loving and kind
And rewards each one of us according to our service to him.

Psalm 63: Parched and weary landscape

O God, my God, I search for you in the desert,
In a parched and weary landscape,
In the dry and burning wilderness,
I thirst for your presence.
For your love is better than life itself
And I will praise and bless you all my days.
I contemplate how much you have helped me in the past,
I meditate on your love and generosity.
I will follow closely in your footsteps,
And you will gather me under the shadow of your wings.
You will protect me from evil
And I will rejoice and trust in God.

Psalm 64: God will act

Lord, hear my supplications,
My plea that you should act to save my life.
For the ungodly wait to ambush the innocent,
They set traps in secret.
They plan their evil crimes
And think the Lord does not see them.
But God will act and bring them to ruin,
He will show himself as mighty and powerful.
Then everyone will stand in awe
And confess the greatness of God.

Psalm 65: Confident in the Lord

We wait on the Lord and offer up our praise and prayers.
All people will turn to you, O God, ready to unburden their sins,
Confident that you will hear their pleas and forgive their transgressions.
O God, you are the hope and delight of all the world.
You formed the mountains and quietened the raging seas.
At dawn and dusk you paint the skies with your glory
You make the world fertile and bless its growth with soft rain.
The hillsides and valleys blossom with gladness, the lambs skip with joy.
The bounty of the earth resounds with ecstasy at the goodness of the Lord.

Psalm 66: Saved our ancestors

Make a joyful sound to the Lord; sing to the Lord all the earth.
How wonderful, how awesome are your deeds, O God
Your enemies flee before you and all the earth sings praises to your name.
See what glorious miracles God has performed
How he saved our ancestors by parting the sea for their escape,
How he brought us out of times of tribulation,
Through fire and flood, to our promised land.
I will keep the vows I have made to you, Lord; I will do what is holy and right.
I have called to the Lord with a pure heart and he has heard me,
He has answered my prayer and I remain in his love.

Psalm 67: Circle the world

O God, bless us with your mercy and love,
Smile down on us and be proud of us,
We will not hesitate to circle the word
To share the good news of your saving grace and power,
Everyone will praise your righteousness,
The nations will lift up joyful songs in your honour.
Praise God and give him thanks for the bounty of the earth
And the abundance of the harvest.
From near to far, for neighbour and stranger,
Rejoice for the blessings of our God.

Psalm 68: The earth shook

Drive away your enemies, God,
Rise up and scatter them like tumbleweed in the wind
Watch them disperse like smoke that vanishes into thin air.
So shall evil be overcome in the presence of Almighty God.
The righteous will rejoice and be glad before God for all his blessings,
He is father of the orphan and defender to the widows, for he is holy.
He befriends the lonely and provides justice for prisoners.
When God led his chosen people through the wilderness the earth shook.
He replenished the famished lands and refreshed his inheritance.
The Lord commands and the enemy is scattered.
What a glorious God who bears our burdens and gives us our salvation.
He gives us freedom from sin and rescues us from death.
The great and solemn procession of God my King moves forward,
Singers lead the way, and then comes the sound of drums and tambourines
All combine in their loud and joyful praises to the Lord.
Let all God's people praise the Lord and join this royal and holy progress.
All the kingdoms of the earth sing their adoration and bow before God,
They all acknowledge the power and authority of God.
His majesty shines out for all to see.

Psalm 69: Out of my depth

Save me from drowning, God, I am out of my depth and can find no safe foothold.
I am exhausted from weeping; my throat is hoarse from calling to you,
My eyes are weak from looking so long for my God.
You know all my faults, all the mistakes I have made,
Do not let my foolishness be held against those who put their trust in you.
For your sake, Lord, I have suffered much,
I am mocked and reproached, plotted against and scorned.
Now is the time for you to answer my prayer, Lord
Rescue me from the mire that threatens to engulf me,
Show your mercy and loving kindness to me.
Come for me quickly, Lord, for my spirit has been broken by the harshness of my enemies,
And I long for some sign of pity and compassion.
Wreak your vengeance on those who persecute me.
Release me from my poverty and pain and I will sing your praises,
The humble will be uplifted, as will all who seek God.
Let all the earth praise him, the seas and everything in them.
For God will save Jerusalem and refresh his inheritance.
All who love the Lord shall live in safety and fellowship.

Psalm 70: In deep trouble

Rescue me, Lord, hurry to my side, deliver me from my plight.
I am in deep trouble and can see no escape without your help.
When you have released me, your followers will be filled with joy,
Those who love you will exclaim what a wonderful God you are.
You are my help and my deliverer; bring me your salvation now, Lord.

Psalm 71: Trusted since my birth

Lord, let me find a safe haven with you, where you will listen to my pleas for justice.
Be a rock for me, where I will always be welcome, safe from my enemies.
You are the only hope I have, I have trusted in you since my birth,
Yes, you have been with me from childhood, my constant guide and companion.
Many wonder at my success but it is through your mighty protection that I prevail,
I will praise and honour you all day long because of all that you have done for me.
Do not forget me now that I am old; do not forsake me now my strength is failing.
My enemies will soon see my weakness if you abandon me now.
There have been so many times when you have rescued me from danger.
I praise your name abroad for all your support and the justice you have meted out.
O God, you have been my teacher from my youth and I sing your praises still.
Now I am old and grey-headed do not give up on me, give me time,
Time to tell the next generations about the wonderful things you do,
Time to tell them about your power and justice and loving kindness.
You have let me sink down deep, submerged in so many problems and worries,
But you will haul me up again, up from the blackness of those depths,
You will build me up and comfort me; you will honour me with your love.
I will sing of your faithfulness, O Holy One, I will shout your praises for redeeming me.
I will happily talk all day long about your justice and goodness.

Psalm 72: Reign Forever

O God, give wisdom to those in authority,
May they administer justice to all your people and compassion to the poor.
Let the mountains and hills flourish and the people prosper
Defend the cause of the marginalised and give deliverance to the needy
So they will praise your name for as long as the sun and moon appear in the skies.
May your Son reign throughout all generations
May he be as the refreshing and life giving rain that falls on the earth
Helping all good people to flourish and peace to abound.
May he have dominion over all, from sea to sea, coast to coast.
May all peoples bow down before him and serve him.
He will show compassion to the hungry and poor
He will wipe away every tear and give encouragement to the faint hearted.
He will intervene to end violence and hatred and bring salvation to all.
And he shall live. He shall live and his name will be honoured forever.
There will be life and food in abundance, throughout the land
And his people will bless him throughout every day.
Blessed be the Lord our God who does wonderful things,
Let the whole earth be filled with his glory.
Blessed be God forever and ever, Amen!

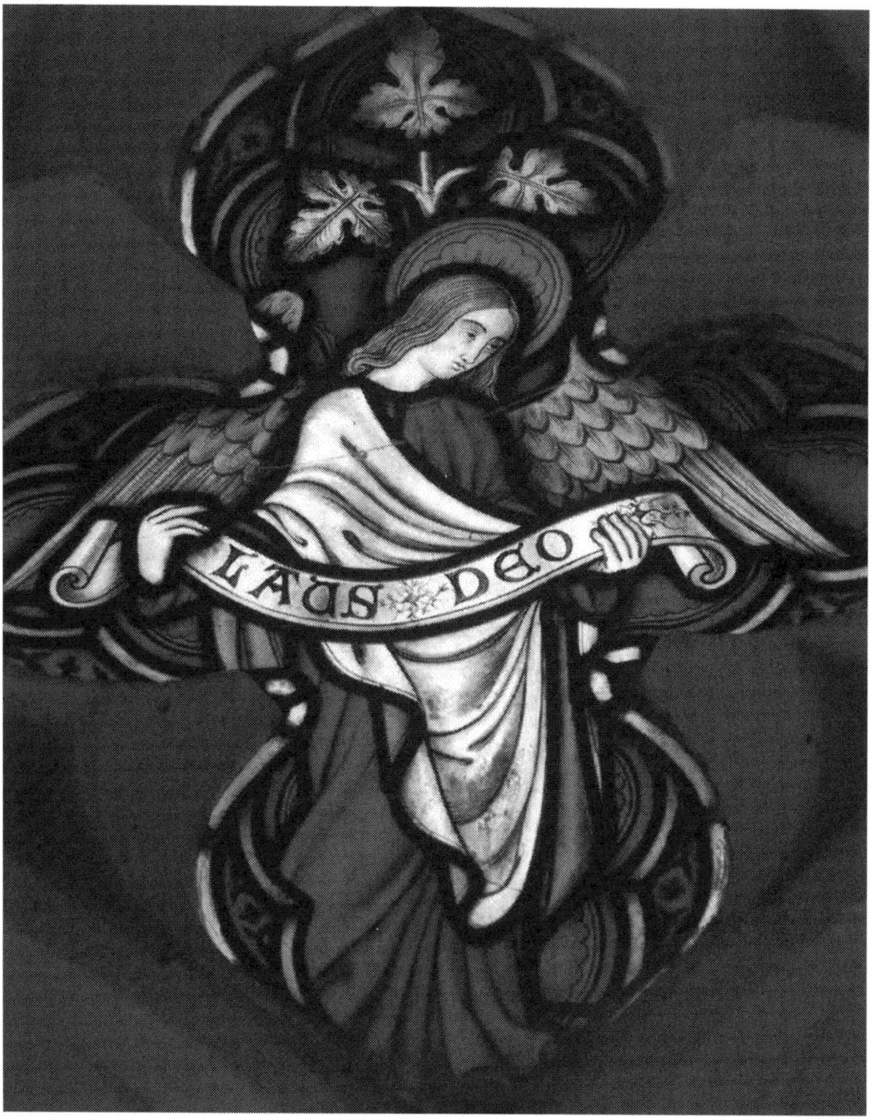
LAUS DEO

Psalm 73: Those who would lead me astray

How good is God to the pure in heart, the upright and the faithful.
But as for me, I was almost lost, teetering on the edge of oblivion!
I envied the prosperity of those who would lead me astray,
Their smooth talk and easy boasting caught my attention.
Their self confidence and self regard shone out like a bright jewel.
With taunting and slanderous words against God and his works,
They lead their admirers on and parade their wickedness.
People are dazzled by their decadence and comfortable living.
This is what the wicked are like and they go on increasing their wealth.
Does this mean I have been wrong to keep to the straight way,
Wasted my time trying to stay pure and innocent?
I have been wracked by temptations whilst keeping to such a regime
But if I had uttered my distress I would have betrayed the trust of God.
I did not fully appreciate all this until I entered the house of the Lord.
There, in safety and serenity, I began to understand the fate of the wicked.
They are balancing on the edge of a precipice and God will cast them down to ruin,
Putting an end to all their pretence and the spectacle of their arrogance.
When I realised this, I saw clearly the folly of my former ways,
But despite my past, despite all my transgressions, God still loves me,
He guides me and supports me with his wisdom and good counsel
I may have times of doubt and weakness but God will be my strength and my redeemer,
It is wonderful to be close to God, he is my refuge,
I will not cease to tell of his marvellous deeds.

Psalm 74: All nature obeys

O God, why have you forsaken us, why are you so angry with your flock?
Remember, you once lead us out of slavery and made us your people.
We return to a sanctuary that has been desecrated by our enemies,
Everything lies in ruins, everything we once held dear and venerated.
Their policy was to destroy and obliterate any trace of God and his people,
How long, O God, will you allow our enemies to dishonour your name.
An arrogant nation has blasphemed your name, why do you hold back?
God, you are my King and the leader of your people from ages past.
You divided the Red Sea by your strength to give them a path to freedom,
You wrestled with demons and evil spirits to bring peace to the wilderness,
You commanded springs of water to gush forth in the dry desert to slack their thirst.
The day and the night belong to you, the starlight and the sun,
All nature obeys your wishes, the summer and the winter as well.
O Lord, save me, protect the dove from the hawk, the weak from the wild beast.
Remember your promise to us; we need your light to shine in this dark land again,
Your down-trodden people have been insulted for long enough,
We need your urgent help to rebut the shame we suffer from these cursed enemies.

Psalm 75: Warned

We give thanks to you, O God,
Your mighty miracles show how much you care.
God says, the time will come when I will judge the earth,
I will punish the wicked.
The insolent and the arrogant have been warned,
For God will bring justice,
His judgement will be poured out over sinners
And every drop must be accepted,
The cup of righteousness shall be drained to the dregs.
I will sing praises to the God of our ancestors,
The strength of the wicked will be soaked away
But the strength of the righteous shall overflow.

Psalm 76: Greatness beyond our imagination

God, you are known and respected by your people for what you have done,
Your greatness is beyond our imagination, more majestic than the mountains,
Awesome and mighty, you conquer our enemies with ease.
No one can stand before an angry God.
Your fearful justice makes the earth tremble.
You decide between good and evil
And vent your wrath on sinners.
People of God, make your peace with the Lord,
Worship at his feet and seek his forgiveness,
For his arm is mighty and his vengeance terrible.

Psalm 77: With outstretched arms

I cry out to the Lord again and again,
I lift up my hands in my desperate pleading
There can be no relief for me until the Lord acts.
Through the dark, depressing night I pray to God,
My comfort is in thinking about the days of the past,
The many miracles and kindnesses he did for me,
With outstretched arms he welcomed me to his home.
I meditate and search my spirit for what has changed.
Has the Lord now rejected me? Have I lost his love?
Is the distance between us now so great that I am forgotten?
O God, your ways are holy and true, awesome in your power.
The Red Sea trembled at your approach,
The skies heaved with thunder and rain,
The lighting cracked and lit up the world,
The earth shook to its very core.
You have redeemed the sons of Jacob and of Joseph by your might,
You lead your people to safety, like a shepherd leads his flock.

Psalm 78: Promises

Listen to what I have to teach you, the story I have to tell,
The history of former generations, the lives of our ancestors.
When you have this knowledge you will be able to tell your children
About the glorious and mighty deeds of our God.
For He gave us His laws and commanded that they be taught to each new generation
And so his laws are passed down through the years.
In this way we have God's word handed on to us,
Our inheritance is his love and mercy and the hope He has set before us,
Not like some of our ancestors who stubbornly rebelled against God.
Some people forgot all that God had done for them and refused to follow His ways.
God who divided the waters and led their forefathers to safety by day and by night,
He split the rocks in the wilderness to give them fresh water in a parched land.
Yet they kept up their rebellion, continuing to sin against God,
They were not content and wanted more in their greed.
God heard their grumbling and was angry and yet He still rained down manna.
He sent them the very bread of heaven for food,
Directed the winds and caused great numbers of birds to fall for them to eat.
He gave them all they wanted and the people ate their fill,
But the anger of the Lord then rose against them,
He sought His vengeance and brought death to the strongest of them.
Even this was not enough to bring the people back into obedience,
So He cut their lives short and gave them years of terror.
Then they spoke their repentance and flattered him,
They remembered that God was their rock and salvation,
But their hearts were not in their supplications,
They did not keep their promises.
Again and again He forgave them and showed his compassion.
He remembered they are only mortal, gone in a moment like a breath of wind.
But still their rebellion continued, bleak years that grieved God's heart,

They turned away from God and denied His saving grace.
They forgot his power and all He had done to rescue them in the past.
The plagues and disasters He had meted on their enemies,
The pestilence and disease, the death and destruction sent on their people and lands.
He gave free course to His anger and did not spare the Egyptians.
Then God helped His people to escape and led them like a shepherd to the Promised Land
Through the wilderness, He kept them safe,
Held back the sea for them to pass,
Before it closed in upon their pursuers.
He kept his promises and brought them to his land of blessings,
He drove out those who occupied the land
And settled the tribes of Israel in their apportioned homes.
And still they rebelled, regardless of God's graciousness to them,
They back from the Promised Land and turned away from God's will.
It was then that God finally turned away from them
He surrendered his glory into the hands of the enemy.
He stood back whilst His people were attacked and murdered,
Young men burnt alive and young women killed,
The priests slaughtered and their widows dead before they could grieve.
Then the Lord awoke from His anger and drove back His enemies.
Then God made his decision about who should lead his people,
He chose the tribe of Judah and built His temple on Mount Zion.
God chose David to be the shepherd of His people
To guide them and tend for them with an upright heart.

Psalm 79: Help us

O God, your country has been invaded by the ungodly,
They have defiled your holy places, ravaged your sanctuary.
Your followers have been cut down, their bones pecked clean by birds of the air
The flesh of your faithful servants taken by wild beasts.
Innocent blood has been spilt and runs like water in the streets
There is now no one left to even bury their bodies.
We are mocked by our neighbours at our weakness.
O God, will your anger with us last forever?
Could you not turn your wrath upon the godless nations rather than us?
On those that do not call upon your name, those that refuse to pray?
They are the destroyers of your people.
Do not hold us to account for the transgressions of our ancestors,
Show your compassion to us, show mercy in our time of extreme need.
Help us, O God of our salvation, remember your promises and save us.
The heathens dare to boast that we have no God to protect us,
Put right this slander and avenge the deaths of your faithful servants.
Hear the groans of your suffering people and strike vengeance on your enemies,
Then shall your people, the flock of your pasture, give thanks forever and ever
Your praises will be sung from generation to generation.

Psalm 80: Let your face shine upon us

Good shepherd of your chosen people, bend your ear and hear my plea,
Show your mighty power and beauty,
Bring salvation and hope to your people who are in great distress.
Return us to your bosom, O God,
Encircle us with your joy and love.
Only in this way can we be saved.
Our prayers have not pleased you,
You have answered us with sorrow and tears
And we are the laughing stock of our neighbours.
Return us to your bosom, O God,
Let your face shine upon us,
That we may be saved.
You took great care to bring us from Egypt,
You treated us like a tender vine when you planted us in your promised land.
Like a good gardener, you cleared the ground and tilled the soil,
We took root and flourished in your estate.
We reached to the mountains,
We became as established as the mighty cedar trees,
We stretched our presence from the sea to the river.
Why, then, have you broken down our walls and left us with no protection?
The wild beasts are upon us.
We beg you to return, O God, and bless us.
Look down and see the plight of your vine!
Protect what you yourself have planted,
This son you have raised for yourself.
Strengthen the one you love,
The son of your choice.
Then we will never turn away from you again,
Give us life and we will put our trust in you.
Return us to your bosom, O God
Let your face shine upon us
And we will be saved.

Psalm 81: Relieve our weary shoulders

God makes us strong and so we sing his praises,
With the sound of tambourine, lyre and harp
And the playing of trumpets in a feast day fanfare
For God has given us these joyful times
To celebrate and remember our escape from Egypt.
I heard a forgotten voice say He would relieve our weary shoulders,
Free our hands from their heavy tasks.
He reminded me that He had saved us when we cried out,
He had brought us out of the land of Egypt,
He had tested and supplied us when there was no water to drink.
The voice said the people of God must never bow down to any foreign god,
They must never worship idols.
If only the people of Israel would turn and listen to this forgotten voice of God,
Every blessing would be possible again.
But do they want to listen? Do they think they know better?
If only Israel would listen to God, follow in His paths,
How quickly would they find salvation!
A strong and faithful people fed with the love of God.

Psalm 82: Judgement

God has taken his place in the court of judgement,
Amongst those who hand out justice to their fellow citizens.
He sees that they refuse to listen to the evidence,
They give special favour to the unworthy.
They ignore their responsibility to give justice to the weak and the destitute,
To give support to the orphan and the afflicted,
To rescue the needy from the grasp of evil men.
But those judges have no wisdom or integrity,
They walk in darkness, without the light of God in their lives.
They think themselves mighty but they are all mortal,
Death will soon greet them, as it will any prince.
Rise up, O God, deliver your judgement on the earth
For all the world belongs to you,
All nations are in your hands.

Psalm 83: Don't walk by

O God, speak up! Don't walk by in silence.
You must surely hear the tumult and commotion of your enemies.
You can see what they are doing, these proud men who hate the Lord.
They show themselves for what they are,
They make cunning plans against the righteous
And conspire together in their rebellion against you, Lord.
They are resolved to utterly destroy the nation of Israel, to wipe out any memory of it.
We are surrounded on all sides by enemy peoples who are in evil league against us.
But you, God, know well how to deal with such cowardly attackers
You have prevailed over your enemies before, fertilised the soil with their corpses.
O my God, scatter them like chaff before the wind, like dust kicked in the air,
With smoke and flame, burn them like a forest fire roaring across the mountainside.
Pursue them and terrify them with your wroth and vengeance.
Show your mighty arm so they see how futile and puny are their efforts.
Let them learn that you are the true God and in charge of all the earth.

Psalm 84: A single day in your presence

How lovely is the house of God, O Lord of heaven and earth.
I long to enter your courtyard, I faint with the expectation of being in your presence,
My joy will be in the living God.
Sparrows and swallows are free to nest at your altars,
Happy are those who find a place in your company and ever sing your praises.
Happy are those who are strong in you, Lord, and who want to follow your steps.
When they take the path through the valley of sorrows,
It becomes a place of bright springs and sweet pools,
Bringing blessings and refreshment and they grow from strength to strength.
O God, hear my prayer. Listen to Israel, Lord, our defender and shield,
Have mercy on your anointed, your chosen King.
A single day spent in your presence is worth a lifetime,
I would rather sit at your feet than live in the palaces of the ungodly.
For the Lord God is our light and our salvation,
He bestows goodness and justice
And, by His grace, we walk beside Him on life's journey.

Psalm 85: Salvation at hand

Lord, you are generous to your people,
You have poured out rich blessings on the land,
Restored the fortunes of Israel and pardoned our sins,
Your anger and your wrath have been satisfied,
May it never rage against us again.
Help us to return to your loving presence,
So that we will stay ever faithful to you, O Lord.
Revive us and redeem us as your children for all generations,
Then your people will rejoice in you forever.
Pour out your steadfast love and grant us your salvation.
I will pay careful attention to what the Lord says,
For He will speak peace to His people,
To those whose hearts are true, those who do no sin.
His salvation is at hand to all who worship and adore Him.
Yes the Lord pours down His blessings and the land is made bountiful
His pathway is paved with justice and truth.

Psalm 86: God of compassion and forgiveness

Bend your ear to hear my prayer, Lord,
Answer me for I am poor and needy.
Protect your obedient servant,
Have mercy on your devoted follower.
I worship you in happiness and joy
For you, Lord, are so good and forgiving,
You abound in your love for all who call on you.
Listen to my urgent prayer whenever I am in peril.
I know that you are mighty, you alone are God,
All nations and all peoples will bow down before you,
They shall glorify your name, O Lord.
Teach me your ways that I may walk in your truth,
Make my heart strong to be always faithful to you.
I give thanks to you, O Lord and praise your name,
So great is your love, you have rescued me from the depths.
O God, violent and godless people rise against me
And they will not show mercy to me.
But you, O Lord, are a God of compassion and forgiveness,
Slow to anger and full of loving kindness.
Turn to me and be gracious to me,
Show a sign that I am in your favour,
So that those who pursue me may see this and be put to shame,
Because you help me and comfort me.

Psalm 87: People of Jerusalem

The holy city of Jerusalem stands high and glorious in the
imagination of your people, O Lord.
People are proud to boast of their birth in other cities of the world,
From countries in all points of the earth they will fondly record their
birthplace
But someday, the highest honour will go to a person from
Jerusalem,
God himself has established that this will be so.
This will bring blessings to all those born in the city
And the people shall rejoice and sing: "All my heart is in Jerusalem."

Psalm 88: Lament

O Lord God of my salvation,
Night and day I have wept before you.
Hear and listen to my prayers, in these last days of my life,
My days are full of troubles and death draws near.
I feel as if abandoned on the battlefield, where no mercy is shown,
Abandoned amongst the slain, a hopeless case.
You have put me in the darkest depths,
Your unrelenting anger presses down on me.
My friends shun me, my situation disgusts them.
I am all alone and my eyes are sore with weeping,
Every day I plead for your help, Lord
I raise up my hands to heaven.
Do not delay, Lord.
How can you help me when I am gone!
Do the dead sing your praises, can they proclaim your faithfulness?
Are you known in the deep darkness of the land of forgetfulness?
O Lord, hear me and spare me, this is my constant plea.
It's as if you are happy to throw my life away,
You pay no regard to my plight, you do not watch over me,
I have been close to death ever since my youth
Your wrath has made me desperate and terrified,
It overwhelms me like a flood and I am marooned from your love.
All my friends have gone and I am left in darkness.

Psalm 89: Father God

My everlasting song will be about your love, O Lord,
Every generation shall hear about your blessings,
Surely your steadfast faithfulness will last forever,
Your truth is as enduring as the heavens.
God made a solemn covenant with his servant David,
To establish his descendants as heirs to the throne forever.
Let heaven praise the wonders of the Lord
And all join to praise him for his faithfulness,
For who can compare with almighty God,
All stand in awe of his power and glory
As they gather in reverence around his throne.
The qualities of God are far beyond compare
The very character of God is in his faithfulness.
You still the raging of the oceans by your words,
You scatter your enemies by your awesome power,
The heavens are yours, the world and everything in it,
From north to south, you created it all!
By your mighty arm you formed the mountains,
Your right hand is lifted high in glorious strength.
Your throne is founded on the pillars of justice and righteousness,
Mercy and truth are your faithful attendants,
They walk before you in the joyful light of your presence,
They rejoice all day long and proclaim your holy name,
You are their strength and the very font of their being.
Our protection is from the Lord himself who has given us our King.
God spoke in a vision to his faithful one, his prophet,
Revealing his servant David as the one chosen to be King,
God anoints him with holy oil and promises to be with him always,
To strengthen him and protect him from his enemies.
God vows to beat down his adversaries and destroy those who hate him,
To protect and bless him always and surround him with his love.
King David will be great because of God's steadfast love,
He will acknowledge God as his Father and Rock of Salvation.
God will treat him as his first born and make him the mightiest King.
God vows an everlasting promise to always love and protect him
His covenant is with the house of David for all generations.
But remember, if these future generations turn away from God,
If they forsake his statutes and do not walk in the way of the Lord,
Then they will be punished.

But, like a good parent, they will still be held in the love of the Father,
He will stay true to his covenant and uphold his promise to the line of David,
It shall be like the moon, an enduring witness in the skies.
But why have you now rejected the one you chose to be King?
Have you renounced the covenant made with your servant?
You, O God, have broken down his defences, trampled his crown in the dust.
He has been robbed by every passing stranger and mocked by his neighbours.
His enemies rejoice at their new found strength against him.
You are no longer beside him in battle and his sword is blunted,
His throne is overturned and his days are numbered.
O God, for how long can this go on, for how long will your wrath last?
You make our lives so short, what can we achieve in such little time?
We cannot escape the grave, when we realise everything is empty and futile!
Lord, where is the love you used to show for me?
Where is the promise of steadfast kindness you made to David?
You have left me in a desperate situation, despised and ridiculed by all,
Even though you once set me apart as your anointed King.
And yet, I will remember to bless you Lord forever! Amen and Amen.

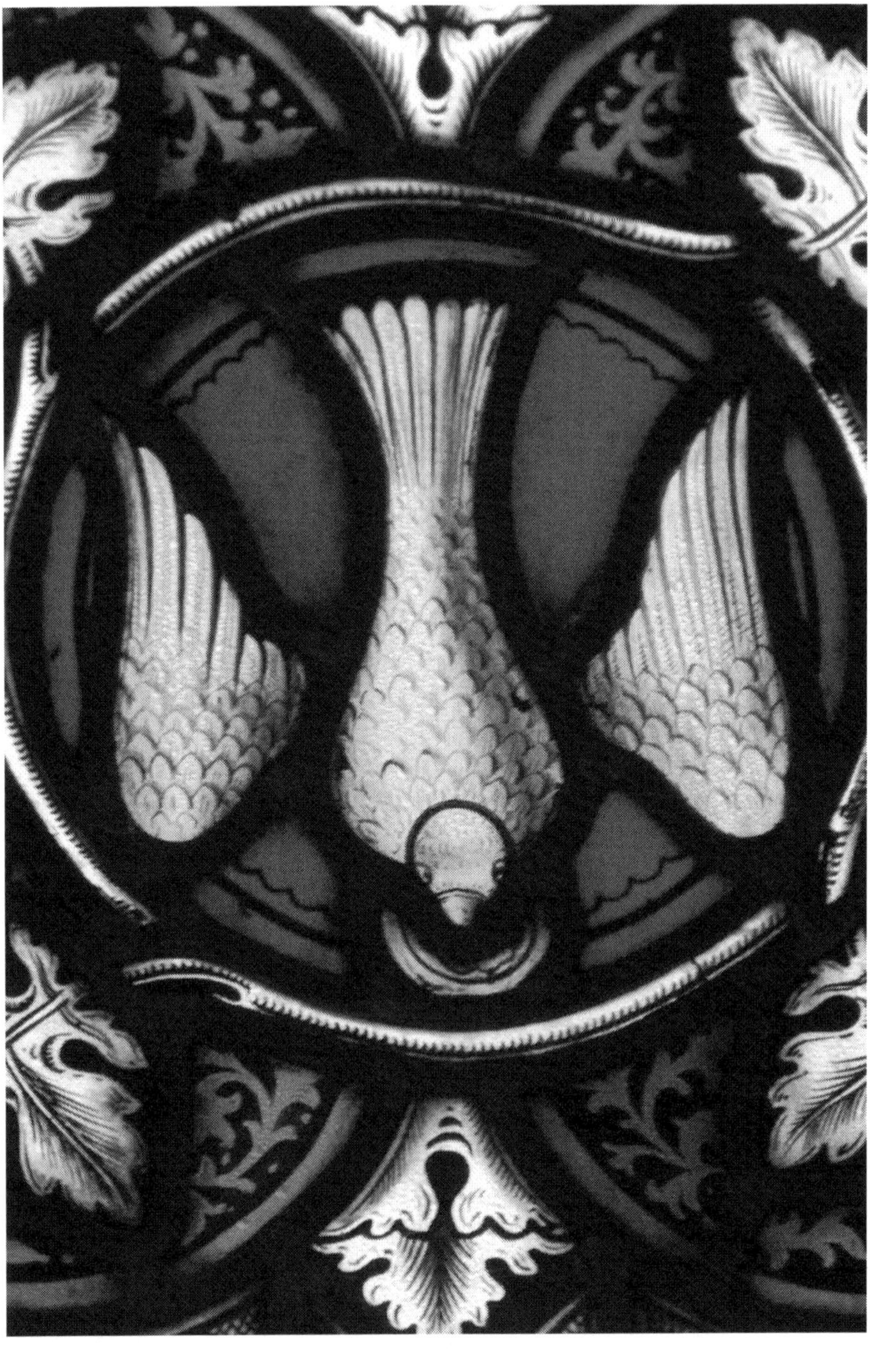

Psalm 90: Trust in God

Lord, throughout all generations we have put our trust in you.
Trusting in a God that has existed for all eternity
From the beginning of creation to the end of time.
At your command, we are turned from dust to dust,
For you, a thousand years are like a passing day.
You brush these hours aside like the cobwebs of a dream,
Like the mown blades of grass that have withered before evening.
We are overwhelmed by your anger, cut down by your wrath,
Spread out before you are all our transgressions, every one of our sins you see,
Our years are long and weary beneath your steely glare,
And all our days are filled with wailing and sighing.
The life you have given us is seventy years, or eighty years if we are strong,
But this span is full of emptiness and trouble and soon it is gone!
Who understands the power of your anger, who pays you proper respect?
Teach us, Lord, to value our days and make the most of what you have given us.
How long will you withhold your blessings on us, O Lord?
Turn away your anger from us; show us again your steadfast love,
May we rejoice and be glad every day, from our youth until the end of our lives.
Match our days of joy and relief to those dark times of misery and affliction,
Work through your servants, Lord, and let us see your miracles again,
Let our children see glorious things and let the favour of the Lord our God be upon us.

Psalm 91: Keep from stumbling

We are sheltered by the love of God
You can trust in the safety of his care.
He will protect you from pestilence
And rescue you from every dark danger.
His faithful promises will be your armour,
For He will shield you from any disasters,
You will be safe in His care, both day and night.
Even in the midst of evil, you will remain untainted,
You will see how the wicked are punished
But you will stay free from sentence,
Because God is your refuge from sin.
God will command his angels to protect you,
They will bear you up to keep from stumbling,
So you do not dash your foot against a stone.
You will be safe even amongst lions and adders.
God has promised to save those who love him,
They can trust in His name and call on the Lord.
He will bring them long life and salvation.

Psalm 92: Sturdy cedar trees

Let us give thanks to the Lord, for it is good to sing his praises.
Remember each morning to thank Him for his kindness,
In the evening, to rejoice in his faithfulness.
Sing your praises with music on the harp and on the lyre,
For you, O Lord, have done such good things and I am glad to sing for joy.
How great are your works, O Lord, how deep are your thoughts!
Your plans and your promises are beyond the comprehension of so many,
They cannot see that although the wicked may flourish now,
They are doomed to eternal destruction.
But the Lord continues forever, exalted in the heavens.
You have made me strong, O Lord, refreshed by your blessings.
I have seen my enemies brought down by your hand,
But the godly flourish like the sturdy cedar trees of Lebanon.
They are planted in the house of the Lord,
And flourish in the courts of our God.
They will produce fruit into old age and stay vital and green.
Like this, the Lord is upright and he is my rock.
There is nothing but goodness in Him.

Psalm 93: Mighty and powerful

The Lord God is King over all; He is robed in majesty and girded in strength,
The world is His and all that there is in it and this is how it has always been.
All creation thunders out its praise to God, the seas roar and the floods lift up their voice.
You, Lord, are mightier and more powerful than the waves, more majestic than the waters.
Your royal commands cannot be changed, holiness is the key of your reign.

Psalm 94: Vengeance

Lord God, rise up in your vengeance,
Let your glory shine forth in your judgement of the earth.
Sentence the wicked as they deserve so they no longer boast of their sinful ways.
In their insolence they pour out their arrogant words,
They crush your people, O Lord and oppress your inheritance,
They attack and murder widows, immigrants and orphans,
They say the Lord does not see and does not care!
They are so foolish; do they think that God who made the ear does not hear?
Do they think that God who formed the eye does not see?
He who planted the nations and kept them within bounds will also discipline you,
He knows everything, what you are thinking and what you are doing.
The Lord is fully aware how futile and weak is humankind
That He must discipline us and teach us to follow His paths,
Give us respite whilst He pursues the battle with our enemies,
For the Lord will not forsake His people, they are his possession,
Judgement will again be true and all the godly will rejoice.
Who will protect me from the wicked?
Who will be my champion against the evildoers?
If the Lord had not been there to help me when I was slipping,
If He had not reached out to save me, I would have been lost.
When doubt and fear fill my mind, you are there to bring calm and trust,
Surely you can have no truck with corrupt government,
You cannot permit wrong to defeat right
Or approve of those who condemn the innocent to death.
No! The Lord is my mighty rock, my fortress,
He will repay the wicked for their infamy
And destroy them by their own plans,
The Lord God will wipe them out.

Psalm 95: The people of His pasture

Come, let us sing a joyous song to the Lord, our rock and our salvation.
Go before Him with thanksgiving and jubilation,
For He is a great God and King of all creation.
He controls the depths of the earth to the mightiest mountains,
He made the sea and formed the land, all is his,
Kneel before the Lord our Maker!
He is our God and we are the people of His pasture, the sheep of his land.
Listen to the voice of your Shepherd, O Israel, do not harden your hearts towards Him,
Do not test the Lord your God as your ancestors did in the wilderness.
For forty years that generation strayed from the ways of God,
They were loathed by God and were not allowed to enter the Promised Land.

Psalm 96: Confess Him as God

Sing a new song to the Lord, all the earth join in this song of praise,
Sing to the Lord and bless His holy name, tell of His goodness every day,
Proclaim his glory throughout the earth, the amazing things He does,
Great is the Lord and greatly to be praised and revered,
His holiness is beyond compare, as is the might of His intent,
Honour and majesty surround Him; strength and beauty are His domain.
Worship the Lord, O nations of the world, confess Him as God.
Honour Him with your promise of pure and holy lives.
Tell all the nations that God reigns and He will judge the people with fairness,
Let the heavens be glad and let the earth rejoice,
Let this be seen in the roaring of the oceans,
The exultation of the fields and the praise of trees and forests,
For the Lord is coming to judge the earth,
He is coming to judge the nations with justice and truth.

Psalm 97: Let the earth rejoice

The Lord is king, let all the earth rejoice, be glad!
He is surrounded by a thick dark cloud,
Justice and righteousness are the foundation of His throne.
Flames go before Him and consume His enemies,
The world is lit up by His lightings and the earth trembles,
The mountains melt like wax at the coming of the Lord.
The heavens proclaim His perfection and all people behold His glory.
All who worship images and idols are disgraced, they must bow before Him.
All Israel has heard of your justice, Lord, and are glad,
For you are most high over all the earth and reign in majesty.
The Lord loves those who hate evil,
He protects those who are faithful to Him,
Rescues them from the clutches of the wicked.
Light dawns in the lives of the godly, bringing goodness and joy.
Rejoice in the Lord and give glory to His holy name.

Psalm 98: Praise for God

Sing to the Lord a new song of praise,
For He has done most marvellous things,
For He has won a mighty victory, by His blessed power.
The Lord has announced His victory and revealed it to every nation,
He has maintained His promise to show mercy to His people Israel
And so the whole earth has seen God's salvation.
The whole world breaks forth in praise for God,
Sing your praises with music on the lyre,
Let the trumpets and horns join in with these joyful sounds.
Let the seas crash on the shoreline with glee,
Let the floods clap their hands,
Let the hills sing together their songs of joy before the Lord,
For He is coming to judge us all with perfect justice.

Psalm 99: The power of the Lord

The peoples tremble to know that the Lord is King,
He sits amongst the Angels, let the whole earth shake.
The Lord is great in Zion, exalted over all peoples and rulers,
Let them hold your name in great reverence.
Mighty God, lover of justice,
You have made fairness the basis of everything you do,
You administer righteousness throughout Israel,
Exalt the Lord our God for He is worthy of praise.
He has answered the calls of His prophets,
He spoke to them and they followed His instructions.
O Lord our God, you answered them and forgave their sins,
Yet punished them when they went astray.
Exalt the Lord our God and worship at His holy mountain,
For the Lord God is holy.

Psalm 100: Confidence and joy

Make a joyful shout for the Lord, all the earth,
Obey Him with gladness in your heart,
Come before Him with confidence and joy.
Know that the Lord is God, His authority stretches over all,
He made us and we are His, the sheep of his pasture.
Enter His fold with thanksgiving in your heart,
Approach Him with praise and humility,
The generosity of the Lord is overflowing
His steadfast love is constant and everlasting
His faithfulness is true for all generations.

Psalm 101: The pure and blameless path

My song for you, Lord, will be of your justice and loyalty,
I will happily sing in praise of your loving kindness.
I will endeavour to walk the pure and blameless path
But I must call on your help to guide me, especially at home,
So I can turn my eyes away from anything base,
And avoid the temptations and smears of evil doers.
I will not tolerate anyone who undermines their neighbours,
I will not permit conceit and pride.
I will welcome the faithful into my home,
Only those who are not stained by sin shall be in my favour.
The deceitful shall be cast out of my house,
I will shun those who tell lies and spread falsehoods.
Morning by morning I will root out the ungodly from the city
To cleanse the streets of the city of God.

Psalm 102: Prayer for renewal

Lord, hear my prayer, let me cry out to you in my distress,
Bend your ear to my plea for an answer to my troubles.
My days are disappearing like smoke in the wind
And I feel my body burning up inside,
My health is trampled and broken, my heart is sick,
My food is like ashes in my mouth, I have no appetite.
I am skin and bones, groaning in despair,
All alone in a desert wilderness, forgotten and abandoned.
I am taunted by my enemies, they use my name as a curse.
My face is lined with the tears of my crying for you, O Lord,
Because of your anger against me, because of your wrath,
For you who once lifted me up have now thrown me out.
Now my life is passing into the evening shadows
And I wither away like dried up grass.
But you, O Lord, will be King forever and for all generations,
Surely you will show mercy and compassion to Jerusalem
For it is the right time to shine your favour on her,
Your people hold the city in high regard, they treasure it's very essence,
Let the nations fear the name of the Lord for He will rebuild Jerusalem,
He will answer the prayers of the destitute,
He will appear amongst them in his glory.
Let this be recorded for future generations,
So that they will praise the Lord for all that He has done,
How he looked down from on high and heard the groans of his people in slavery,
And he set them free so that the Lord will be worshipped in Jerusalem,
With his praises sung throughout the city and beyond.
But now, in my middle age, God has sapped my strength,
How can the Lord do this to me when he will live forever,
Forever and yet I will die half way through my allotted span.
Long ago, you laid the foundations of the earth
And with your hands set the heavens in their place,
Even they will perish but you will go on forever,
They will decay and collapse like an ageing sun
And you will form new bright stars in the firmament.
But you yourself never grow old, never diminish,
You are forever; your years have no end.

But the line of your peoples will continue,
All generations will be preserved by your faithfulness.

Psalm 103: God's love

Bless the Lord, all that is in me, bless His holy name,
I will not forget all the wonderful things He has done for me.
He forgives all my sins; He heals the disease within me
And saves me from hell by surrounding me with His love.
By his influence, my youth is renewed like the eagle's!
God gives justice to all in need of His compassion and forgiveness,
He made known His ways to Moses and the people of Israel.
He shows tender mercy to those who deserve it,
Slow to anger and full of kindness and love.
He is gentle and forgiving to His people
And has not punished us as we deserve,
His mercy is as boundless as the heavens above.
He has separated us from our sin as far as east is from west.
He is our father, tender and loving, understanding of our needs and desires
He knows what little time we have, that we will soon be gone,
Soon wither like the flowers in the field, like the wind that ruffles the grass and leaves no trace,
He remembers that we are but dust.
The steadfast love of God is everlasting for those who are faithful to Him,
To those who abide by his holy covenant and obey him in future generations.
The Lord has established His authority in heaven and earth,
He reigns in majesty and power from on high,
Bless those who listen carefully to His commands and administer His wishes.
Let heaven and all creation bless the Lord,
Bless the Lord all that is in me, bless His holy name.

Psalm 104: Wonderful creation

I bless the Lord my God, how great and powerful you are,
Clothed in majesty you shine through your universe,
A pure and holy light that illuminates your creation,

From the star studded canopy of space to the depths of the seas,
The very elements of wind and fire obey your commands.
You embrace the world, you hold us all together.
You covered the earth with the oceans and the mountains above,
At the sound of your voice these mighty foundations were formed,
The seas were contained so they will never cover the earth again.
You have placed springs in the valleys and rivers to flow from the hills,
Water for animals and a place for birds to nest in the trees along their way.
You refresh the earth with rain, the grass grows and the fruit flourish,
You feed the cattle and we cultivate the ground for our food and wine,
See the ancient trees planted by the Lord, their majestic height,
Where birds build their nests and storks find a home amongst the firs,
In the high mountains you have provided pastures for the wild goats,
And amongst the rocks there is protection for wild animals.
You have set the moon to mark the months and the seasons,
The sun to mark each day with its rising and setting,
You have created the darkness when the creatures of the forest are about,
The young lions roar for their food but they obey you, O Lord,
At dawn they return to their dens to lie in wait for the night.
People go about their work until the shadows of evening return.
O Lord, what a rich variety you have made, the earth is full of your glory.
Before me lies the mighty ocean, teeming with life of every kind,
There go the ships and over there the whales you have made leap in the waves.
All your creation looks to you to give them food in due season,
You open wide your hands in bountiful provision to satisfy their needs.
But if you turn away from them, they are dismayed,
And when you take away their breath, they die and turn again to dust.
Through your Spirit, new life is created and you renew the face of the earth.
The earth trembles at your glance, the mountains spout flames at your touch.
I will sing to the Lord as long as I live, to my very last breath,

May the Lord be pleased at my rejoicing in his works
May my meditation on his greatness be pleasing to Him.
Let sinners and all who deny God, perish,
But I will bless and praise the Lord.

Psalm 105: Faithful God

Let us give thanks for all that the Lord has done,
Sing His praises and tell everyone about His wonderful works.
Glory to His holy name; let everyone who has given their heart to God rejoice!
Seek always for the love and strength of the Lord,
People of Israel, descendants of God's servant Abraham,
Remember the mighty things He has done and the justice He has delivered.
The Lord our God sits in judgement over all the earth,
He will never forget the promise He made to His people,
The land of Canaan set aside for the descendants of Abraham and Isaac,
A covenant made when the tribe of Israel were but few in number,
Of little account and dispersed among the nations,
But He would not allow any King to oppress them,
Warning them not to harm his anointed ones.
He summoned up famine against the land, cutting off its supply of food,
He sent Joseph ahead of them, who was sold as a slave to Egypt,
His feet shuffling in fetters and his neck in a collar of iron,
His patience was sorely tested until God's time finally came.
Then the pharaoh sent for Joseph and set him free,
He was put in charge of all of pharaoh's possessions,
With authority over all his household.
Then Jacob, who had lived as an alien in his own land, came to Egypt,
In the following years, the people of God, multiplied in number,
God made them stronger than their foes.
At this point, God turned the hearts of the Egyptians against the Israelis,
They hated and enslaved them.
Then God sent His chosen servants Moses and Aaron to lead His people to safety.

Following the instructions of God, they called down miracles of terror upon the land of Egypt.
They caused thick darkness to settle over the land
The waters were turned into blood and the fish poisoned,
The land was plagued by a swarm of frogs, even in the chambers of the pharaoh.
Moses spoke and there came swarms of flies and other insects through the land,
He sent hail and lightening to spoil the land and terrorise the nation
He broke their vines and fig trees, all the trees lay ruined on the ground.
At his command, a swarm of locusts descended on Egypt,
A swarm beyond number that devoured all the vegetation in the land, all the crops,
Then God struck down all the first born of their land, their pride and joy.
Moses then led God's people out of the land of Egypt, together with their gold and silver,
They left in safety and the people of Egypt were glad for dread had gripped their hearts.
God spread a cloud over them to shield them from the sun,
He made a pillar of fire to guide them through the night,
They asked for food and he provided quail and manna,
He caused water to gush out through a fissure in the rock,
It flowed though the dry dessert like a river,
For God remembered his holy promise to Abraham.
So the Lord brought His joyful people into the Promised Land,
He gave them land that had been occupied by other nations
And they ate the crops that others had planted.
This has all been done so that we can be faithful to our faithful God,
And obedient to his laws. Praise to the Lord!

Psalm 106: God's rebellious people

Praise the Lord for he is good and His love endures forever,
The extent of your good works is beyond measure,
Happy are those who find justice and are compassionate to others.
Remember me, O Lord, when you are blessing and saving your people,
Help me also, when you are delivering others from their troubles,
That I may rejoice in their joys and share in their salvation.
We have sinned in all generations, now and in the past,
Our ancestors, when they were in Egypt, did not appreciate God's miracles,
They did not remember the abundance of his love,
But rebelled against him when they reached the Red Sea,
Even so, God stayed faithful to his word and saved them from their enemies,
He divided the Red Sea and made a dry path for their escape,
And then the waters returned and covered their adversaries so that not one survived.
After this, God's people believed His words and finally sang out His praises.
But how short was their memory of these great deeds, how shallow their loyalty!
Very soon after this they tested God in the wilderness, demanding more food,
He gave them the nourishment they wanted but also sent disease to punish them.
They were jealous of the leaders He had chosen, Moses and Aaron,
In response, the earth opened and swallowed Dathan, Abiram and his friends,
Fire fell from the heavens to consume these wicked men.
For they preferred to worship the image of a calf rather than the Glory of God,
They had forgotten God was their Saviour,
Who had done such mighty things in Egypt and at the Red Sea.
God said he would destroy them for such wickedness,
But Moses stepped forward into the breach,
And begged God to turn from his wrath and not destroy them.
Then they would not enter the Promised Land as they had lost faith in the covenant
They grumbled in their tents and would not obey God's commands.
God said he would let them perish in the wilderness,

He threatened to scatter their children into exile.
But then our forefathers joined the worshippers of Baal
And even offered sacrifices to the dead.
This provoked God's anger and a plague broke out upon them.
This continued until Phinehas interceded, for which good deed he will be long remembered.
At the waters of Meribah they again angered God, causing trouble for Moses,
Nor did Israel destroy the nations in the land as God had commanded
But instead they mingled with the heathen and learned their evil ways,
Being led away from God and into worshipping idols.
They even sacrificed their sons and daughters to the demons,
Shedding innocent blood and polluting the land with evil,
Their love of idols was abhorrent in the sight of the Lord,
He let the heathen nations crush them and rule over them,
People of Israel oppressed and enslaved by their enemies.
Many times God rescued them from their slavery,
But they remained rebellious, brought low by their iniquity.
God heard their cries for help and responded to their pleas,
He remembered his promises and showed His compassion,
Even his enemies were persuaded to show pity on them.
Lord God, draw us back from our exile so we can rejoice in your holy name,
Blessed be the Lord the God of Israel, from everlasting to everlasting,
Let all people say, Amen!

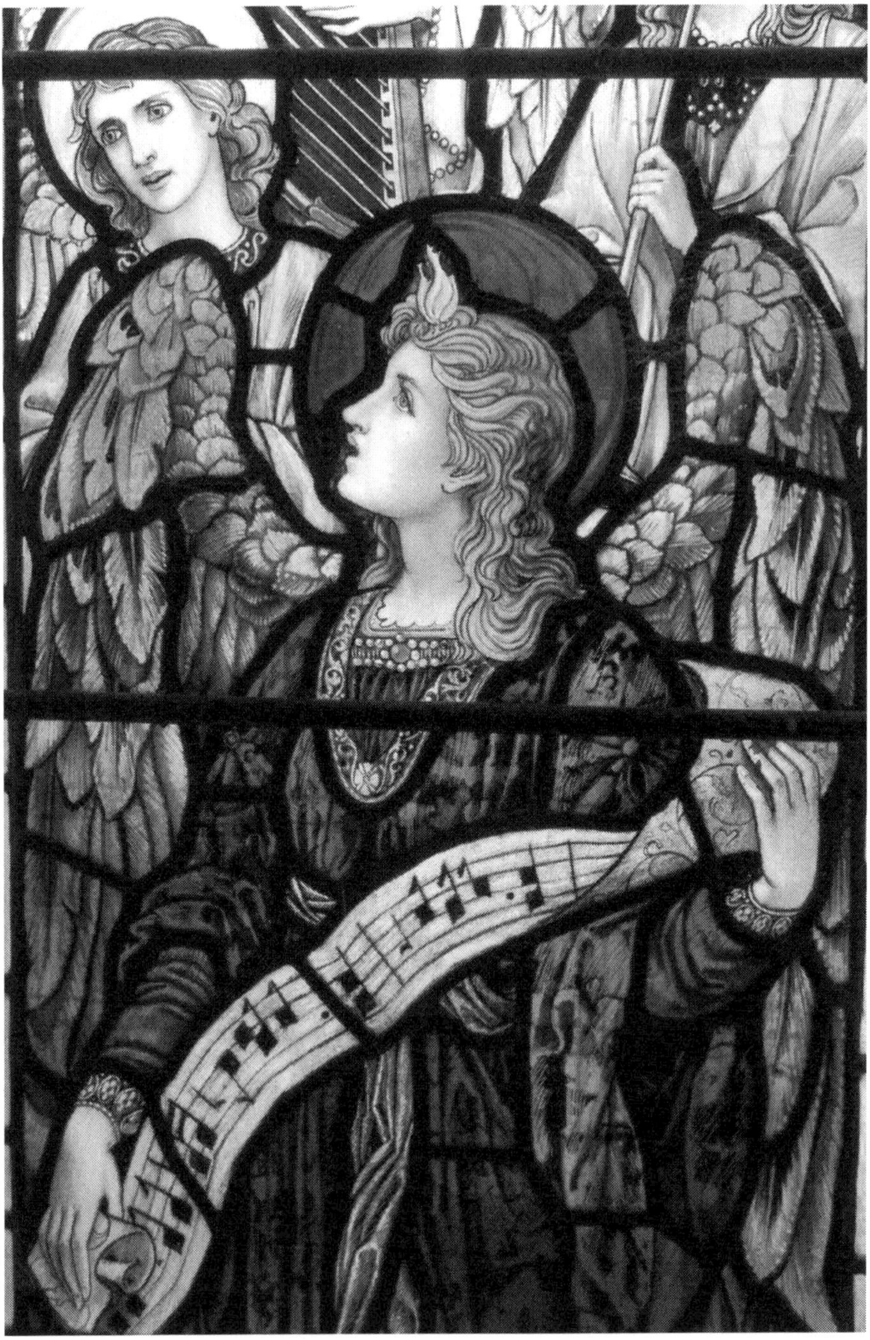

Psalm 107: Everlasting love of God

Let all people say thank you to the Lord for His goodness to us,
Those who have been redeemed speak up for all to hear.
He gathered in the exiles from east and west, from north and south.
Some were found wandering, hungry and thirsty in the wilderness,
Lost and weary, they cried out to the Lord, and He heard them!
He led them by the straight path to safety and a place to live,
Let them praise God for His loving kindness, for all He has done for humankind,
For He refreshes the thirsty and fills the hungry with goodness.
Some sat in darkness, in the shadow of death, in deep misery and slavery,
They had rebelled against God, scorning His authority and power,
Their hearts bowed down with hard labour, they fell and no one could help them,
Then they cried out to the Lord and He heard them in their distress,
He rescued them from the gloom and tore their bonds asunder,
Let them thank the Lord for the compassion He has shown,
For He broke down the prison gates and cut apart the iron bars.
Some were sick because of the sinful lives they led,
They had no appetite for food and they were fast approaching death,
Then they cried to the Lord in their distress and He helped them,
He spoke and they were healed, saved from the door of death.
Let them give thanks to the Lord for His steadfast love,
Sing out their praises and dedicate their worship to a merciful God.
And some went to sea in ships, plying their trade on the oceans,
They saw the wondrous works of God on the deep,
He beckoned to the stormy winds and lifted the boiling waves
The ships were tossed about like matchwood, high and low,
Their courage gone they reeled and staggered across the deck,
Then they called to the Lord in the wreckage of their lives,
He made the storm subside, rescued them and brought them safely into harbour.
O that these sailors would thank the Lord for saving their lives,
Let them sing their praises before the congregation and the leaders of the nation,
God dries up the land of the wicked and turns rivers into deserts of salt.
For the hungry and deserving He replenishes parched land with springs of water,

Where they can settle with fields and vineyards that will flourish and multiply,
They will raise large families and their cattle will thrive.
Others will become poor through oppression, trouble and sorrow,
For God pours contempt upon the haughty and sends them to wander in the wastelands,
But He raises up the poor who are godly and ensures their prosperity.
Good people will recognise this whilst the wicked will be struck silent.
Listen and learn what God is doing and thank Him for his faithful love.

Psalm 108: Prayer for victory

O God, my heart is steadfast in its love for you,
I will sing and rejoice before your throne.
I will wake and sing your praises at the rising sun
The harp and the lyre will make the melody.
Every nation will praise your holy name,
For your loving kindness is for everyone
And your faithfulness reaches to all your creation.
Let your glory stretch over the whole earth,
Hear the cry of your beloved child,
Rescue me with your mighty power.
We exult God for His holy promises to us
He has promised to give us all the land of Shechem,
And portion out the Vale of Succoth,
Also His are Gilead and Manasseh
Ephraim is His helmet, Judah His sceptre,
But Moab and Edom are despised,
And He will shout triumph over the Philistines.
Who but God can defeat the fortified cities of the wicked?
Who else can lead me to the safety of Edom?
Lord, stay with us in our trials against our enemies,
We need the help of God because we are useless on our own,
Together we can show great valour and God will tread down our foes.

Psalm 109: Retribution!

Do not stand silent and apart from us, O Lord,
While the wicked and deceitful gang up on me,
Spreading their slander against me for no reason.
I show my love for them but even while I am praying for them,
They are trying to destroy me,
They return evil for good, hatred for love.
Don't they realise how it feels?
Let them face false witness and come to court before a biased judge,
Let the judgement be to pronounce them guilty,
Their very prayers counted as a sin.
May their years be few, let them be usurped by others,
Let their children be orphans and their wives widows,
Evicted from the ruins of their homes.
May their property and possessions be seized by creditors
Their names blotted out for future generations.
Show no kindness, show no pity for their situation.
Punish the sins of the father and the mother,
Let the name of their family be cut from the memory of the earth,
For they refused all compassion to others and persecuted those in need.
They loved to curse others, now, Lord, you should curse them,
Cursing is a way of life for them, like food and drink,
Now may those curses return to cling to them like the clothes on their backs.
Let the Lord punish my enemies for their lies and threats of death.
As for me, Lord, treat me as your child, one who bears your name,
Show your compassion to me and deliver me from evil.
I feel myself slipping towards death,
Shaken off from the sleeve of life like the dust that we are.
My body is weak from fasting; I have become skin and bones,
I am an object of derision and failure to all.
Help me, O Lord my God, hold out your saving hand to me,
Let everyone know that you are victorious.
Then let them curse me if they like, for you will bless me,
They will be shamed and I will rejoice and give thanks to the Lord.
Make them fail in all their evil endeavours, clothe them with disgrace,
I will give loud thanks to the Lord, praising him to everyone,

For he stands up for the needy to save them from persecution and death.

Psalm 110: The chosen one

Almighty God said to his Son, the Messiah,
"Sit at my right hand and I will subdue your enemies,
To make them bow low before you."
God has established your throne,
From where you will rule over your enemies.
Your people will hurry to follow you on that day,
And all will be new and fresh like the morning dew.
God has sworn that this will be so,
In the priestly line of Melchizedeck.
God stands at your side to protect you,
He will strike down the ungodly in His day of wrath,
He will punish the nations and fill them with their dead,
He will follow the path of righteousness
And be refreshed from its springs along the way.

Psalm 111: He feeds us with love and hope

Praise the Lord; let me proclaim the goodness of God,
Let everyone reflect on His wonderful works,
Everything He has done for us, His majesty and grace.
Who can forget the wonders He performs,
He feeds us with love and hope,
And never forgets His promises to us.
Through His generosity He has given His people the land of Israel,
Though it was the home of many nations living there.
He is faithful and just in all He does,
His laws are formed from truth and goodness and will last forever.
He has rescued His people from slavery
And now nothing will stop them from coming to the Lord.
How can we be wise without the love of God?
For growth in wisdom comes from obeying His laws.
Praise His name forever!

Psalm 112: Trust in God

I cannot tell you how blessed are those who trust in God,
Happy are those who delight in doing His commands.
Their children will be honoured everywhere
They will prosper and there good deeds will be remembered.
When darkness comes, light will burst forth for the righteous,
Kind, merciful and generous are they that serve the Lord.
The godly will never be overcome by evil tidings,
For they are secure in their love of the Lord,
Their hearts are steady, they will not be afraid.
In the end they will prevail over their enemies.
They are unstinting in their giving to the needy,
Their influence and good deeds will never be forgotten,
They will be held in high honour,
The wicked see this and are angry and jealous.
They gnash their teeth and slink away, their hopes thwarted.

Psalm 113: God's goodness

Servants of the Lord, praise His holy name,
Blessed be the name of the Lord, now and evermore,
Praise Him from sunrise to sunset,
High above the nations, His glory is far greater than the heavens.
None can compare with God, enthroned on high,
Far above the heavens and the earth,
Yet He stoops to raise the poor from the dust and the hungry from the bins,
He rescues the needy and sets them amongst princes.
He gives children to the childless wife so she becomes a happy mother.
Praise the Lord!

Psalm 114: History of God's power

A long time ago, when the people of God escaped from Egypt,
The promised lands of Judah and Israel became their new home.
The Red Sea made way for them; the River Jordan shelved its waters,
The mountains skipped with joy, the hills gambolled in ecstasy.
Why did the sea part? Why did the river become shelved?
What was the jubilation felt by mountains and hills, the Rams and the young sheep?
Tremble, O earth, at the mighty presence of God,
He made fresh water gush forth from flinty rock.

Psalm 115: The true God

Yours be the glory, as our living God, not us,
Through your steadfast love and faithfulness,
We praise your holy name.
How dare the nations say you are dead!
Our God is in the heavens, powerful and active,
Their idols are merely human concoctions of gold and silver,
They have no senses; they cannot speak, see, hear, taste or touch.
Those who make and worship them are just as useless.
O Israel, trust in the Lord, He is your shield and defender,
O house of Aaron, trust in the Lord, He is your helper,
All of his people, trust in the Lord, He is your saviour.
The Lord has us in His mind and on His heart,
He will bless the people of Israel and the priests of Aaron,
And all people will bow down before Him.
May the Lord bless you and your children,
May you be blessed by the Lord who made heaven and earth.
The heavens belong to the Lord but He has given the earth to all humankind.
The dead cannot sing praises to the Lord, but we can!
Let us praise the Lord from this time and forever more!

Psalm 116: Saved from death

I love the Lord, for he hears my prayers and answers them,
He bends down low enough to hear every prayer I breathe.
I felt death was very close; I was frightened and scared,
Then I called on the Lord to save me, to save my life.
The Lord is gracious and good, kind and merciful,
When I was brought low and facing death, He saved me.
Now I can be calm for the Lord has healed my anxiety,
Yes, I am safe and secure within His presence.
In my turmoil, I thought I was being led astray,
But now I see I must give my thanks to the Lord,
I will lift up the cup of salvation and call on His holy name,
I will make my vows openly in the presence of all His people,
I know His love is faithful to us, even unto death.
O Lord, you have freed me from the bonds of death,
I am your servant and I will worship you forever,
I will make my vows to the Lord before all his people,
I will pay what is due in the courts of the house of the Lord,
Praise the Lord.

Psalm 117: Call to Worship

Let our praises to God echo throughout all the earth,
Let every nation extol His holy name.
Great is His love towards us all,
The faithfulness of the Lord endures forever,
Praise the Lord!

Psalm 118: We will rejoice and be glad in it

Give thanks to the Lord for all his goodness to us,
His love for us endures forever.
Let the congregation of Israel praise Him,
Let the priests of Aaron praise Him,
Let all who love God praise Him,
And acknowledge His loving kindness is forever.
Out of my distress I prayed to the Lord,
He answered me and He led me from darkness to light,
With the Lord by my side, how can I have any fear?
I will surly triumph over those who would harm me.
It is better to trust the Lord than to rely on mortals,
Better to find refuge in God than an allegiance with base princes!
Though the forces of hatred are encamped around me,
I will march out under the banner of God and defeat them.
They swarm around me like wasps at their nest,
They spit and blaze like fire amongst thorn trees,
Yet, with God's protection, I will prevail.
The Lord is my strength and a song in the heat of battle
By His victory I have gained salvation.
There is much rejoicing in the homes of the godly at this news,
The strong arm of the Lord has done mighty things,
And I shall live to tell of all His marvellous deeds.
The Lord has punished me but He has saved me from death.
Open the gates of righteousness that I might enter to praise God,
Open the gates that lead to the Lord that all may enter.
I thank you, Lord, for rescuing me, in answer to my prayer,
The stone once rejected has now become the cornerstone of your kingdom.
This wonderful event is how the Lord meant it to be.
This is the day that the Lord has made,
We will rejoice and be glad in it.
Save us and help us, O Lord, we beseech you,
Blessed is the one who is coming, the one sent by you, in your name, Lord.
The Lord is God and by his light we see how to serve and worship Him.
You are my God, you know me and I give you my thanks and praise,
O give thanks to the Lord God for He is good and His mercy endures forever.

Psalm 119: The law of the Lord

Those who follow the laws of God are blameless and happy,
Happy are all those who seek Him with a pure heart and do His will,
Who reject evil but walk joyfully in the ways of God.
O Lord, you have laid down your laws and require that we are obedient to them,
May my footsteps be resolute and true in the paths that I will take,
Then I will able to hold up my head and fix my eyes on your commands.
I will praise you with an upright heart as I learn the lessons you have for me,
I will strive to obey you in all things, do not forsake me, Lord.

By following your word, Lord, young people will stay on the path of righteousness.
I have tried my best to find you, Lord, do not let me stray from your commandments.
I have studied you words and treasure your promises in my heart,
Be my teacher, Lord, as I recount your decrees on my lips,
I rejoice in your words more than in riches,
I meditate on your statutes and fix my heart on your ways,
I will delight in them and will not forget them.

Have mercy on me, Lord, that I may live and obey your laws,
Open my eyes that I might understand the power of your word.
I am but a pilgrim here on earth, show me the way to go,
Your commands are my chart and compass, my guide in alien lands.
You rebuke those who wander from your commandments,
Don't let them pour scorn on me for being faithful to your instructions.
Even princes plot against me but I will remain true to your ordinances,
Your decrees are my delight; your statutes are my counsellors.

I am completely discouraged, I lie in the dust of deep despair,
Revive me, Lord, by your holy word.
When I confessed my ways, you heard my prayer and answered me.
Now give me your commands, your orders,
Make me understand what you want of me,

So I can see the glory of your works.
I weep with sorrow, I am stricken with grief,
Your word will lift me up and raise my spirit.
Shield me from error and teach me your law,
For I have chosen the way of truth,
I set your ordinances before me,
I walk in the light of your commandments,
For they enlarge my understanding.

Teach me your laws, Lord, and I will obey them,
Train me in the correct observances and I will be your faithful student.
Guide me along those paths I should take and I will find delight in the journey.
Bend my heart to your will and not to selfish gain,
Keep my eyes on what is true and what is pure,
Reassure your servant that I can trust in your promises.
Save me from being mocked for obeying your laws,
For your laws are right and good.
I long to obey them!
Therefore, renew my life, Lord, as you have promised.

Lord, let your love come to me,
Bring me salvation as you have promised,
Then I shall have an answer for those who taunt me.
May I never forget your words, they are my only hope,
I will keep obeying your laws forever and ever,
Finding freedom within the limits of your ordinances,
I will speak of the value of this to the powerful
And they will listen with interest and respect.
Your commands have been my delight because I love them,
I hold your commandments in reverence and they will order my life.

Remember your word to your servant, O Lord,
Your promises which gave me so much hope.
The arrogant and ignorant hold me in contempt,
But I do not give up in my obedience to God.
From my youth I have tried my best to obey your laws,
Your word has always been my comfort.
I am indignant that the wicked should forsake your law,
Your statutes comfort me wherever I make my home,
Even at night, I think of your holy word,

It is a blessing for me that I have kept your commands.
I submit to God and I promise to obey His word,
Be merciful to me, O Lord, according to your promises.
Looking back, I have not always walked in the way of the Lord,
Wicked men have tried to ensnare me and drag me away from you,
But I am determined to follow the right path now,
I am firmly resolved to stay anchored to your laws.
Even in the middle of the night I will rise to praise you,
I am in fellowship with all who love and worship you, Lord,
The earth is full of your steadfast love,
Teach me to follow your holy ways.

I am overflowing with your blessings, Lord,
Just as you promised it would be,
Now teach me good judgement and wisdom,
For your commandments are my guide.
Before I sought your forgiveness, I went astray,
But now I am true to your word and obey your commands,
You are good and do only good, help me to follow your example.
Proud men have put a slur on my name but the truth is I obey your laws,
Their minds are dull and stupid but I love you with all my heart.
After your punishment of me, I have emerged stronger than before,
Your actions taught me to pay attention to your laws,
Your word means more to me than gold and silver.

By your hands you formed my very being,
Now give me understanding to heed your laws.
All those who trust in you will welcome my company,
Because I am also faithful to your word.
I know, O Lord, that your decisions are just,
And that my punishment was in order to do me good.
Now comfort me, O Lord, with your steadfast love,
I long for your love, the promise of your consolation.
Let the arrogant be shamed in their deceit,
Let your faithful join me in our commitment to your laws,
Help me to love your statutes and be blameless in my devotion.
I yearn for your salvation and yet I know from your promises it will be mine,
My eyes are straining to see the arrival of your good news,
When will you comfort me with your help?
I have become shrivelled like an old wine skin in the smoke,

But I have not forgotten your statutes, O Lord.
How long must your servant wait?
How long before you punish those who persecute me?
They have prepared deep pits for me to fall in,
They flout your laws and their lies have brought me great trouble.
They have almost put an end to me but I have not forsaken you, Lord.
By your great mercy, spare my life, Lord, so I might do your will.

Your word, O Lord, stands firm and immutable in the courts of heaven,
Your faithfulness lasts from age to age, like the earth you created,
By your wish it continues to this day, for all things exist to serve you.
If I had not rejoiced in your word I would have perished in despair.
I will never forget your laws for they give me life,
Save me, for I am yours, I have striven to live according to your wishes.
The wicked lie in wait to destroy me but I will keep my mind set upon your will,
I have seen that worldly perfection has it's limit but your command is boundless.

Lord, I love your word and I set my thoughts on them all day long.
Your commandments make me wiser than my enemies,
They are my constant guide as I ponder your will for me.
I have stopped myself from going along evil paths, in abeyance to your word,
I have not turned away from the ordinances you have taught me.
Your words are sweeter to me than the taste of honey in my mouth,
Your words give me wisdom and understanding and I hate every false way.

Your holy word is a lamp to my feet and a light to the path ahead.
I have sworn an oath to observe your laws,
Lord, I am close to death, give me back my life as you promised.
Accept, Lord, my offerings of praise and teach me your will.
Though my life may hang in the balance, I do not forget your word,
The wicked have set their traps for me but I will not turn aside from your path.
Your will is my joy and treasure forever,
I am determined to observe your laws and follow your wishes until I die.

I despise those who are left in two minds about your word, Lord,
My choice is clear, I love the Lord my God, my shield and my refuge,
Your promises are my only source of hope.
Get away from me all who do evil,
Don't try to stop me from obeying the will of God.
My hopes are founded on your promise that I shall live, Lord,
Hold me safe from my enemies and I can continue to follow your wishes.
You cast out all those who stray from your laws,
All the wicked of the earth you count as nothing.
I love your will and I tremble before your power and authority.

Do not leave me at the mercy of my enemies for I have striven to do what is right,
Give me your blessing, Lord; do not let the proud overpower me!
I am weary waiting for your salvation and the fulfilment of your promise.
Lord, deal with me kindly and teach me your ways,
Give me an understanding of how to apply your word to everything I do.
Lord, now is the time for you to act for the wicked have violated your laws,
I love your commandments more than the finest gold,
I set my way by God's word, whatever it may bring.

Your laws are excellent and I am pleased to obey them.
As your words unfold the light up my understanding of your purposes,
I am amazed and delighted at your plan for us, I cannot wait!
Show mercy to me, Lord, as you show mercy to all your followers,
Keep my steps guided by your promise, let no evil divert me from my path,
Save from those who would oppress me that I may keep to your will,
Look on me with love and teach me your laws,
I am distraught that your laws are not obeyed by all.

O Lord, you are holy and your judgements are fair,
Your decrees are perfect and just.
I am angry because my foes have no regard for your word.
Your promise endures and so I can rely on it,

Even though I am of little consequence, I do not forget your wishes.
Your justice is eternal and your law is truth.
Through trouble and anguish, your word has comforted me.
Your laws are always fair, help me to appreciate this and I shall live.

With my whole heart I want to assure you, Lord, I will obey your laws.
I cry out for you to save me, Lord, so I can do your will.
I rise before dawn and put hope into my words of prayer,
I lay awake at night, thinking about your promises.
In your love, hear my voice, O Lord, and make me well.
Those who persecute me are drawing near, the ridicule your word,
Yet you, Lord, are close and all your commandments are true.
Long have I known that your will never changes.

Look down on my misery and rescue me for I remember your law.
Save me and give me back my life just as you have promised.
The wicked are far from salvation for your laws are alien to them.
Great is your mercy, Lord, give me life according to your justice.
Though my enemies are so many, I do not swerve from your way,
I am disgusted by the faithless because they care nothing for your laws.
See how much I love your word; give me back my life and health,
Your word is founded on truth and every syllable is for eternity.

The powerful persecute me with no reason while I stand in awe of your word,
I rejoice at your word like one who has found a great treasure.
I hate and detest all falsehood but I love and cherish your laws.
I will praise you seven times a day because of your wonderful laws.
There is great peace and confidence to be found in your word.
I long for your salvation, O Lord, and I fulfil your commands.
I keep your laws and I love them dearly,
I obey your will and all my ways are open to you, Lord.

O Lord, listen to my prayers, teach me your ways as you have promised,
Hear my prayers and rescue me as you said you would.
I will not cease from praising you for the privilege of learning your laws.
I will sing about their wonder for each of them is just.
Be ready to help me, Lord, for I have chosen to follow your word.

I have longed for your salvation and your law is my delight,
Let me live that I might praise you; let your word save me.
I am as a lost sheep; find me Lord, for I do not forget your word.

Psalm 120: Peace and war

In my troubles I cry to the Lord that He may answer me.
Deliver me, O Lord, from liars and the deceitful.
What should happen to those with a treacherous tongue?
They should be pierced with arrows and burned with glowing coals.
I live in an alien land and my troubles grow amongst these haters of the Lord,
Too long have I lived amongst those who hate peace.
I call for peace, but when I speak, they talk of war.

Psalm 121: Watchful day and night

Will it be from the mountains that my help comes?
No, my help comes from the Lord who made heaven and earth,
He will save me from stumbling and will stay watchful day and night.
The Lord is your constant shield and defender, ready at your right hand.
He will keep you from all evil and preserve your life,
Wherever you go, the Lord will see you are safe, now and forever.

Psalm 122: Prayer for peace in Jerusalem

I was glad when they said let us go to the house of the Lord.
Now our feet are standing inside the walls of the city,
Inside the gates of Jerusalem where your people gather to worship,
In accordance with the edicts set out in your laws, O Lord.
Pray for the peace of Jerusalem, so that all who love you prosper,
May there be peace within your walls and safety under your roofs,
I ask this for the sake of my brothers and friends who live there.
May there be peace as a protection over the House of the Lord.

Psalm 123: Prayer for mercy

Ruling over all creation, I lift my eyes to you, O Lord,
We look to our God for His mercy and kindness,
Just as a servant always looks to their master.
Have mercy on us, Lord, have mercy,
For we have had enough of setbacks,
Enough of scorn and contempt from the rich and proud.

Psalm 124: Thanks for salvation

Israel knows the truth,
If the Lord had not been on their side,
They would have been swallowed up by their enemies,
Destroyed by their anger, drowned beneath the raging waters of fury and pride.
Blessed by the Lord who has saved us from such terrors.
We have escaped being the prey of our detractors,
Like a bird set free from the hunter's snare.
Our salvation is in the Lord who made heaven and earth.

Psalm 125: May the good prosper

Those who put their trust in the Lord are like Mount Zion, strong and everlasting,
Just as the mountains around Jerusalem defend the city,
So the Lord surrounds his people, now and for evermore.
For this land is allotted to the righteous, not the wicked,
And the godly shall never be drawn into doing wrong.
O Lord, do good to those who are good,
May they prosper all who love you.
But drive away those who follow evil and crooked ways.
Let peace rest upon Israel!

Psalm 126: Thanks for deliverance

When the Lord delivered His people from bondage, it seemed like a dream,
We were filled with laughter and our lips sang for joy.
Even the heathen acknowledged that the Lord had done great things.
Indeed, the Lord had done great things for us and we rejoiced.
Refresh us and restore our fortunes, O Lord, as streams in a dry land.
Those who started in tears will burst forth in joy,
Those who go out weeping, carrying the seed for sowing,
Shall return home singing with joy, carrying their sheaves.

Psalm 127: God's blessings

Unless the Lord builds the house, we labour in vain,
If the Lord does not watch over the city, we are in peril.
There is no sense in working long hours into the night
For God gives his people blessings whilst they slumber.
Children are a gift from God, they are his reward.
Children of one's youth are like arrows to a warrior,
With a full quiver you can be supported and defended,
All the help you need, when speaking with your enemies.

Psalm 128: The blessings of home

Blessed are they who love the Lord and walk in His ways.
Their reward will be prosperity and happiness.
Your wife will be content and fruitful within your house,
Your children, healthy as young olive trees, crowding around the dinner table,
This is God's reward for those who love and trust Him.
The Lord bless you from on high all the days of your life!
May you live to enjoy your grandchildren!
Peace be upon Israel!

Psalm 129: Shame on Israel's enemies

Your people have been pressed hard from the earliest days,
They have faced persecution and discrimination but have survived,
But our enemies have never managed to prevail over us.
Their whips cut my back like furrows across a field,
But the Lord is good and releases me from the chains that bound me.
May all who hate Zion be put to shame and defeated,
Let them be like grass in shallow soil that withers before it flowers,
Ignored by the reaper and despised by the binder,
While those who pass by refuse to bless them.

Psalm 130: Wait expectantly for forgiveness

From deep despair I call to you, Lord, hear my cry,
Let your ears be attentive to my pleading, answer me!
Lord, if you only remember our sins, who then will stand?
But you are a forgiving God, ready to show mercy,
For this I praise your holy name and wait expectantly.
I trust in the Lord and hope on His word,
More than those who watch for a new day.
O Israel, put your hope in the Lord for His love is constant,
He has the power of salvation and He will redeem Israel from her sins.

Psalm 131: Quiet humility

Lord, I am not proud or scornful,
I do not think myself above others,
I have not tried to overreach myself
Or occupy myself with matters beyond my understanding.
I am humble and quiet now before the Lord,
Like a young child with its mother.
Yes, my boasting has been stilled.
O Israel, you should quietly trust in the Lord,
From this time and forevermore.

Psalm 132: God's promise to David

O Lord, remember the hardships endured by David,
The oath he swore, the commitments he made to you.
He strove long and hard and suffered many deprivations,
In his efforts to find a permanent place for you, Lord,
A dwelling place for the Mighty One of Jacob.
First, the Ark was in Ephrathah, and then in the fields of Jaar,
But now we will have a place in Jerusalem to worship God.
Rise up, O Lord, and enter your Temple with the Ark.
Let your priests be clothed with holiness,
Let the faithful shout for joy.
Do not reject your servant David, the king you anointed,
You promised that his son would succeed him and sit on the throne,
You said, if they keep your covenant and your laws,
The dynasty of the family of David will last forever.
The Lord has chosen Jerusalem for His home,
This is where He will live forever,
He will bless the city and meet the needs of her poor and hungry,
He will clothe her priests with salvation, her saints with joy,
David's power will grow and his way will be made clear.
God will cover his enemies with disgrace,
But David will shine out as a glorious King.

Psalm 133: Harmony

How very good it is when families live together in harmony,
As precious as anointing oil running down upon Aaron's head,
Running plentifully over his beard and robes.
Harmony is as refreshing as morning dew on the mountains.
God's eternal blessing on the mountains of Israel.

Psalm 134: Bless the Lord

Bless the Lord, all you who serve God,
Those who stand watch every night in the house of the Lord,
Lift up your hands in praise and worship, to bless the Lord.
May the Lord of Zion bless you,
The maker of heaven and earth, bless you.

Psalm 135: Hymn of praise

Praise the Lord; yes, let His people praise Him,
Those who stand in the house of the Lord,
Sing to His wonderful name, for He is gracious.
The Lord has chosen Israel as His own possession.
I can witness to the greatness of the Lord,
His will rules supreme in heaven and earth
And His measure runs to the deeps of the seas.
He causes the mists to rise and sends lighting and rain,
He brings out the wind at his command.
In Egypt, he struck down the firstborn, child and animal,
He performed great wonders in front of the Pharaoh and his people.
He struck down nations in their greatness,
And slew kings in their splendour,
Sihon, King of the Amorites,
And Og, King of Bashan,
And all the kingdoms of Canaan,
And gave their land as a promised gift to the people of Israel, forever.
Your name, O Lord, will endure forever, honoured through all generations,
For the Lord will bring justice to His people, compassion to His servants.
The heathen nations worship idols of silver and gold, made by human hands,
They are made with mouths that cannot speak, eyes that cannot see,
They have ears but cannot hear and they cannot even breathe.
This is the fate for those who trust in idols, they will come to be like them!
House of Israel, bless the Lord!
Priests of Aaron, bless his name!
House of Levi, bless the Lord!
All who love the Lord, bless his name!
All Israel bless the Lord, the God who resides in Jerusalem.
Praise the Lord!

Psalm 136: Litany of praise

Give thanks to the Lord for He is good, for His love endures forever,
Give thanks to Almighty God, for His love endures forever,
Give thanks to the Lord of lords, for His love endures forever.
Praise Him who alone does great wonders, for His love endures forever,
Praise Him who made the heavens, for His love endures forever,
Praise Him who girded the land with seas, for His love endures forever,
Praise Him who made the heavenly lights, for His love endures forever,
The sun to rule over the day, for His love endures forever,
The moon and stars to rule over the night, for His love endures forever.
Praise the God who smote the firstborn of Egypt, for His love endures forever,
Who brought the people of Israel out of captivity, for His love endures forever,
With a strong hand and a outstretched arm, for His love endures forever,
Who divided the Red Sea in two, for His love endures forever,
And led them safely through, for His love endures forever,
But drowned Pharaoh and his army in the sea, for His love endures forever,
Praise the God who led His people through the wilderness, for His love endures forever,
Who struck down heathen nations, for His love endures forever,
And killed famous kings, for His love endures forever,
Sihon, king of the Amorites, for His love endures forever,
And Og, king of Bashan, for His love endures forever,
And give their land as Israel's inheritance, for His love endures forever,
A promised gift to His servant Israel, for His love endures forever.
God remembered us when we were laid low, for His love endures forever,
He rescued us from our foes, for His love endures forever,
He gives food to all His people, for His love endures forever.
Give thanks to the God of Heaven, for His love endures forever.

Psalm 137: Exile

We sat down beside the rivers of Babylon and wept as we remembered Zion.
There can be no more singing; we have hung up our harps on the willows by the water.
But we are taunted by our captors who call on us to sing songs from our homeland!
How could we sing the Lord's song when we are held in a foreign land?
If I forget you, Zion, let me forget my skill in playing the harp,
Let my tongue stick to the roof of my mouth so that I never sing again.
O Lord, do not forget what the armies of Babylon did at the fall of Jerusalem,
The devastation they caused when they captured your holy city.
O Babylon, happy are those who will repay you with the destruction you brought,
To take up your children and dash them against the rocks!

Psalm 138: Thanks and praise

I give you thanks with all my heart, O Lord,
I will sing your praises before all heaven.
I thank you for your steadfast love and faithfulness,
Your name is exulted above all names.
When I pray, you answer me and raise my spirits.
All the kings of the earth shall praise you, Lord,
For all of them shall hear your voice,
They shall sing of the ways of the Lord,
For though you are great, you have regard for the humble,
But the proud are not welcome in your presence.
Though I walk in the midst of trouble,
You protect me against the wrath of my enemies,
You deliver me to walk safely in the way of the Lord.
You fulfil your purpose for me,
For your love endures forever.
Lord, do not forsake the work of your hands.

Psalm 139: You know me, Lord

O Lord, you have examined my heart and you know me,
You know when I sit down and when I rise up,
You know my thoughts, even when you are far off.
You map out my path and plan my journey.
You know where I am at any moment of the day.
You know what I am going to say even before I speak.
O Lord, you know me completely,
Before me and after me you are there,
Your hand is placed as a blessing on my head.
Such reassurance is so wonderful for me.
There is nowhere I could go that you would not be,
Nowhere that your spirit is not also there.
If I ascend into heaven, you are there,
If I go down to the place of the dead, you are there,
If I travel on the morning winds to the farthest seas,
Even there your hand will guide me and support me.
The blackness of night will not cover me from your love
To you, darkness is not dark; it is as light to you.
You made all the inner parts of my body
And knit me together in my mother's womb.
Thank for the intricacy with which you made me,
Wonderful are your works and great is your skill.
You were there before my birth, when I was being formed,
You knew me before I began to breathe,
Every day has been recorded in your book.
How precious to me is the knowledge I am constantly in your thoughts,
O Lord, such blessings are without number.
I call on you to slay the wicked, O Lord,
And drive out the bloodthirsty and malicious from me.
Do I not hate those who hate you, O Lord?
Do I not loathe those who rise up against you?
Yes I hate them, for your enemies are your enemies.
Search me, O God, and know my heart,
Test me and know my thoughts.
See if there is any grain of sin in me
And lead me along the path to everlasting life.

Psalm 140: Call for deliverance

Deliver me, O Lord, from the wicked; protect me from their violence,
Rescue me from those who plan evil and stir up trouble all day long.
Their tongues are as sharp as a snake's and their bite is full of venom.
These proud and arrogant men have set a trap to catch me,
They wait with a net to throw over me and hold me in its meshes.
You are my God, listen to me, O Lord, listen to my pleas,
Don't let these wicked men succeed, don't let them prosper.
You see these evil men, let them be overwhelmed by their own mischief,
Let burning coals fall down upon their heads,
Or else fling them into deep pits where there is no escape.
Do not let their slanderous ways be established in the land,
Punish them quickly, O Lord.
I know the Lord will surely help the persecuted,
He will maintain the rights of the poor.
The godly will give thanks to your name for they shall live in your presence.

Psalm 141: Prayer for protection

Lord, come quickly, in answer to my prayer,
Listen when I cry for your help!
Let my prayer be like incense wafting up to you,
My hands lifted high in evening worship.
Set a guard on my mouth, O Lord,
Keep watch over what I say.
Save me from being tempted by evil ways,
Stop me from mixing with sinners,
Do not let me share in their ill gotten gains.
Let the godly strike me, the faithful reprove me,
Make me take this medicine for my own good.
My constant prayer is against the wicked and their deeds.
When such people are condemned and punished
They will finally listen to my words of counsel.
I look towards you, O Lord, for help.
You are my refuge, do not forsake me.
Keep me safe from their traps and the snares of the wicked,
Let them fall into their own nets, while I escape.

Psalm 14: Feeling trapped

I open my mouth and cry to the Lord,
I plead for mercy and pour out my complaints before Him.
When I am faint hearted you know what I must do,
The path I must take to avoid the traps that have been set.
These snares are close by but no one cares what happens to me.
I cry to you, O Lord, you are my only refuge, only you can save me.
Rescue me from my persecutors for they are too strong,
Free me from the prison of their intimidation so that I can thank you.
The godly will greet me and together we will praise your holy name.

Psalm 143: Needing God's help

Listen to my prayer, O Lord, hear my plea,
Answer me in your faithfulness.
Do not judge me for no one compares in goodness before you.
The enemy that chased me has crushed my life to the ground,
They force me to live in darkness, the darkness of the grave.
My spirit is in a faint and I have lost all hope.
I remember your glorious miracles in days long ago,
I stretch out my hands for you; I thirst for you in a parched land.
Come quickly, O Lord, answer me for my spirit fails,
Do not hide your face from me or I shall die.
Be kind to me in the morning for I put my trust in your love,
Teach me the way to go and I will lift up my spirit to you.
Save me from my enemies, O Lord, now that I have run to you for refuge,
Teach me to do your will, for you are my God,
Stretch out your hand to lead me along good and holy paths.
For the glory of your name, Lord, bring me salvation,
In your holiness and by your promise, lead me out of my troubles,
By your love for me, cut off my enemies and destroy my adversaries,
For I am your servant.

Psalm 144: Prayer of hope

Bless the Lord, who is my rock,
He trains my arms for battle and my hands for war.
He is my rock and my fortress, my tower and my deliverer.
He goes before me as a shield and controls my people.
O Lord, that you should even notice human beings!
Our days are but a breath, a passing shadow.
Lower the heavens, Lord, and come down,
Touch the mountains and make them smoke,
Let loose your lightening arrows upon your enemies, and scatter them.
Reach down from on high and rescue me from the mighty waters,
Save me from the clutch of aliens whose mouths speak lies,
Who swear the truth of what is false.
I will sing you a new song, Lord, with a ten-stringed harp,
For you are the God who gives victory to kings,
Who rescues his servant David from the sword.
You deliver me from these enemies, these liars and treacherous men.
May we have sons as vigorous and tall as growing plants,
Daughters of grace and beauty like the pillars of an elegant palace,
May our barns be full to the brim with produce of every kind,
May our sheep increase by thousands in our fields,
May our cattle be heavy with their young,
May there be no breach in our walls, no exile for our people,
And no cry of distress in our streets.
Happy are those to whom such blessings fall,
Happy are the people whose God is the Lord.

Psalm 145: In praise of God's glory

I will praise you, my God and King,
And bless your holy name forever,
Every day I will bless you,
And praise your name forever and ever.
God is great and greatly to be praised,
His greatness is beyond our knowing!
Let each generation tell its children of your mighty works,
I will marvel at the glorious splendour of your majesty,
Your awesome deeds shall be spoken of by all,
And I will proclaim your greatness.
The people shall celebrate your abundant goodness,
And sing aloud of your righteousness.
The Lord is kind and merciful, slow to anger, full of love.
The Lord is good to us all; His compassion is over all that he has made.
All creation will thank you, Lord, and your people will bless you.
They will tell of the glory of your kingdom and of your power,
They will speak of your miracles, the majesty and glory of your reign.
Your kingdom never ends, and your dominion endures throughout all generations.
The Lord is faithful and gracious in all his deeds,
He lifts the downcast and raises up all who are bowed down.
The eyes of all are fixed on the Lord who gives them their food in due season.
From your open hand you satisfy the needs of every living thing.
The Lord is fair and just in all his doings and full of compassion.
He is close to all who call on His name in truth,
He answers the prayers of all who are faithful to Him,
He hears their cries for help and rescues them.
The Lord watches over all who love Him,
But all the wicked He will destroy.
I will praise you, my God and King,
All flesh will bless His holy name, forever and forever.

Psalm 146: In praise of God's compassion and faithfulness

Praise the Lord,
I will sing praise to my God all my life long.
Do not put your trust in Princes; there is no help to be had from mere mortals,
When their breathing stops, they die and return to the earth,
In a moment, all they planned for themselves comes to an end.
Happy are those whose help is in the God of Jacob,
Whose hope is in the Lord his God,
The God who made heaven and earth,
The seas and everything in them.
He is the God who keeps His promise,
Who gives justice to the poor and oppressed,
Who gives food to the hungry.
The Lord sets the prisoners free and opens the eyes of the blind,
He lifts up those who are bowed down,
For the Lord loves the righteous.
The Lord protects the immigrants,
And cares for orphans and widows.
The Lord loves the just but thwarts the wicked.
The Lord will reign forever, in every generation,
Praise the Lord.

Psalm 147: A song of thanksgiving

Praise the Lord!
How good to sing praises to our God, for He is gracious.
He is rebuilding Jerusalem, bringing back her exiles.
He heals the broken hearted and binds up their wounds,
He counts the stars in the night sky and calls them by name.
Our Lord is mighty; His power is absolute, knowledge unlimited.
He lifts up the downtrodden and casts down the wicked.
Sing out your praises to the Lord, with melody on the harp.
He covers the heavens with clouds and prepares rain for the earth,
He makes the green grass grow on the hills,
He feeds the animals and the young ravens cry for food.
His delight is not in the strength of the horse or the speed of the runner,
His joy is in those who worship Him, those who have hope in His steadfast love.
Praise the Lord, O Jerusalem! Praise your God O Zion!
For He has fortified the gates to your city and has blessed your children,
He sends out peace across your nation and fills your barns with grain,
He issues his commands to the earth and His word runs swiftly,
He sends snow like wool, scatters the frost and hurls the hail on the earth.
Who can stand before His freezing cold?
But then He calls for the Spring winds to blow and the river ice to break.
He declares His word to Jacob, His laws and ceremonies to Israel,
No other nation has been told these ordinances.
Praise the Lord!

Psalm 148: Praise the Lord

Praise the Lord!
Praise Him from the heavens, praise Him to the heights!
Praise Him all his angels, all the host of heaven!
Praise Him, sun and moon and all you shining stars!
Praise Him, skies above, vapours high above the clouds.
Let all creation praise the name of the Lord,
He established them forever and ever and set their bounds.
His orders will never be revoked.
Praise the Lord on earth you creatures of the ocean depths.
Let fire, hail, snow, frost and stormy wind all obey His commands.
Let the mountains and hills, fruit trees and all cedars,
The wild animals and cattle, the snakes and birds,
The kings and all the people, with their rulers and judges,
Young men and girls, old men and children,
All praise the Lord together, for He is worthy.
His glory is above heaven and earth.
He has made His people strong, honouring His faithful ones,
The people of Israel,
Praise the Lord!

Psalm 149: Praise and victory

Praise the Lord!
Sing to the Lord a new song.
Sing His praises, all His people.
O Israel, rejoice in your maker,
Let the people of Jerusalem rejoice in their King.
Praise His name with dancing and music on the drums and lyre.
For the Lord takes delight in His people,
He will crown the humble with salvation.
Let the faithful rejoice in His honour,
Let them sing for joy from their couches,
Let the praise of God be on their lips
And a two-edged sword in their hand,
To execute vengeance on the nations,
And punishment on their peoples.
Bind their kings with fetters and their leaders with chains of iron,
And execute their sentences.
This is justice for His people.
Praise him!

Psalm 150: Surpassing greatness of the Lord

Praise the Lord!
Praise Him in his temple and in His mighty firmament,
Praise Him for His mighty deeds, His surpassing greatness!
Praise Him on the trumpet,
Praise Him with lute and harp,
Praise Him with tambourine and dance,
Praise Him with strings and pipes,
Praise Him with clanging cymbals,
Praise Him with loud clanging cymbals!
Let everything that breathes praise the Lord!
Praise the Lord!

Printed in Great Britain
by Amazon